Ordnance Survey
Exmoor
and the Quantocks
Walks

Pathfinder Guide
Compiled by Brian Conduit

Key to colour coding

The walks are divided into three broad categories, indicated by the following colours:

Short, easy walks

Walks of moderate length, likely to involve some modest uphill walking

More challenging walks, which may be longer and/or over more rugged terrain, often with some stiff climbs

Acknowledgements

I would like to thank Mr B. Pearce of the Exmoor National Park, and Mr J. W. Carslake and Mrs S. Twiss of the National Trust for their valuable advice and assistance. I would also like to thank Derek Earnshaw for re-checking two of the routes.

While every care has been taken to ensure the accuracy of the route directions, the publishers cannot accept responsibility for errors or omissions, or for changes in details given. It has to be emphasised that the countryside is not static: hedges and fences can be removed, field boundaries can alter, footpaths can be rerouted and changes of ownership can result in the closure or diversion of some concessionary paths. Also paths that are easy and pleasant for walking in fine conditions may become slippery, muddy and difficult in wet weather and stepping stones over rivers and streams may become impassable.

Ordnance Survey   ISBN 0-319-00212-8
Jarrold Publishing   ISBN 0-7117-0459-7

First published 1990 by Ordnance Survey and Jarrold Publishing

Ordnance Survey   Jarrold Publishing
Romsey Road   Barrack Street
Maybush   Norwich NR3 1TR
Southampton SO9 4DH

Printed in Great Britain by Jarrold Printing, Norwich. 1/90

Previous page: *Luccombe church and village*

Contents

Introduction to Exmoor and the Quantocks

A land of steep-sided, narrow and bracken-covered combes, wide expanses of grass and heather moorland, spectacular cliffs and headlands and beautiful wooded valleys through which rush clear and sparkling streams. A land of villages, so idyllic and picturesque that they seem almost unreal, in which thatched pubs dispense good food and ale and thatched cottages dispense traditional cream teas that can be so overwhelming that the next modest hill on your route seems like an unattainable mountain peak. This is Exmoor and its neighbouring hills the Quantocks, an area in which the walker really does enjoy the best of all worlds — especially when an extensive and well waymarked network of footpaths is added to this delectable package.

Exmoor National Park is the second smallest in England and Wales (only the Pembrokeshire Coast is smaller) — 265 square miles, of which approximately two-thirds lies in west Somerset and the remaining third in north Devon. Its northern boundary is the Bristol Channel coast, stretching in a dramatic series of hog's-back cliffs, interrupted only by the Vale of Porlock, from North Hill above Minehead in the east to Little Hangman above Combe Martin in the west. On its western and southern borders the moor descends in an arc-like shape to merge into the rolling farmlands of Somerset and Devon, and its eastern frontier is formed by the Brendon Hills. Facing the Brendons, across a fertile valley that runs northwards from the Vale of Taunton Deane to the coast, are the Quantock Hills, a distinctive, broad-backed ridge almost 12 miles (19 km) long, which in turn overlook Bridgwater Bay, the flat lands of the Somerset Levels and the line of the Mendips beyond. When the National Park boundaries were drawn up the Quantocks were excluded; they constitute a separate Area of Outstanding Natural Beauty, though there are many affinities — scenic, geological and historical — between them and Exmoor.

Curving round the southern edges of Exmoor and the Quantocks are a series of market towns that serve as the chief gateways into the region: from east to west these are Bridgwater, Taunton,

Robber's Bridge in the lonely valley of Weir Water

Wellington, Tiverton, South Molton and Barnstaple. Within the region of moorland and hills itself there are just a few small towns — Dunster, Dulverton and Porlock, which are arguably little more than large villages — as well as small villages and coastal settlements.

Exmoor is basically a high and fairly undulating plateau thrust up by primeval earth movements, mostly lying at around 1200 ft (366 m) and rising to its highest point at Dunkery Beacon (1705 ft (519 m)). Both Exmoor and the Quantocks comprise mainly Devonian rocks of sandstone and shales, with the oldest in the north and youngest in the south, with some new red sandstones appearing in the north around Minehead, Dunster, the Vale of Porlock and the lowlands surrounding the Quantocks. In the north the plateau ends abruptly at the line of cliffs that overlooks the Bristol Channel and the coast of South Wales, and is dissected by a series of narrow and steep-sided valleys. Most of the streams from these converge on the sea at one point, Lynmouth, via the gorges of either the West Lyn or East Lyn rivers; hence the terrible flood devastation that occurred there in August 1952, following the exceptionally heavy and persistent rain that fell on Exmoor during that month. The two major rivers of Exmoor, the Exe and the Barle, both rise within two miles of each other on the barren moorland of The Chains and flow south-eastwards, the Barle joining the Exe just to the south of Dulverton. From there the enlarged Exe continues to Exeter and on to the English Channel.

Compared to Dartmoor and the moorlands of northern England, Exmoor is less bleak and forbidding and certainly less extensive; hence the frequent use of such adjectives as 'friendly' or 'benign' to describe it. The only remaining large areas of wild and open country are the grass moorlands of the central heartland — The Chains, Exe Plain and the upper Badgworthy valley, roughly corresponding to the old Exmoor Forest. Here the walking can be as challenging as anywhere in the country and in bad weather is anything but benign. Surrounding this central — or to be exact, west-of-centre — zone are expanses of glorious heather moorland that include such popular rambling areas as Brendon Common, Anstey Common, Winsford Hill and Dunkery Beacon.

The moors themselves are virtually treeless but the valleys contain some splendid broad-leaved woodlands. Some of the finest of these are on lands that formerly belonged to two large estates: the Halliday estate in the valleys of the East Lyn and Hoaroak Water around Lynmouth and Watersmeet, and the vast Holnicote estate of the Acland family to the south of Porlock and around Luccombe and Selworthy. Fortunately both of these areas are now owned and protected by the National Trust. Equally attractive and even more spectacular are the coastal woodlands that extend almost without a break from Porlock Bay westwards to The Foreland, with another superb belt above the aptly-named Woody Bay.

On the eastern fringes of the moor the Brendon Hills provide a different type of landscape: a more gentle and pastoral scene of rolling hills and deep wooded valleys, less bare and open than Exmoor itself, with some arable farming. Some of the slopes are covered by the Forestry Commission plantations of Brendon Forest, and conifers also clothe some of the steep combes that cut into the Quantock ridge, but much deciduous woodland remains as well. Both the Brendons and Quantocks offer excellent walking. A particularly fine ridge path runs along the top of the Quantocks, from Lydeard Hill to Beacon Hill above West Quantoxhead, giving the most magnificent views in all directions.

Of the history of Exmoor and the Quantocks it has to be said that there is really little of any great significance. Important historical events and national developments seem to have passed the region by to a greater extent even than the other remote areas of 'high country' in northern and western England. For much of its history Exmoor has been mostly uninhabited, apart from the valleys and around its fringes, and there are few outstanding physical remains of any historical era. Its prehistoric monuments — standing stones, burial chambers, stone circles and hill forts — are nowhere near as extensive or impressive as those on Dartmoor. The Romans have left little trace apart from two small coastal forts. The Dark Ages are chiefly represented by the Caractacus Stone on Winsford Hill. Dunster's heavily restored castle is the only major reminder of Norman military power in the area. Monastic foundations are almost non-existent, apart from the Cistercian abbey at Cleeve, situated in the fertile vale between the Brendons and the Quantocks. The finest medieval churches are around the edge of the moor, at Minehead, Dunster and Combe Martin. Great country houses are few and far between; Arlington and Nettlecombe are the most outstanding. The Industrial Revolution bypassed Exmoor; even the mineral exploitation that took place in Dartmoor, the Peak District and the North York Moors hardly occurred here, apart from the relatively brief iron-mining boom in the Brendon Hills in the second half of the nineteenth century, when the 'Mineral Line' was constructed along the Washford valley to link the mines to the port of Watchet. From there the ore was shipped across the Bristol Channel to the ironworks of South Wales. Probably the most impressive single historic monument in Exmoor is the clapper bridge across the River Barle at Tarr Steps, the finest and most elaborate of its kind in the country. Its precise age is a mystery: it dates at

Valley of Hoaroak Water – Hoar Oak Tree is in the centre of the picture

least from the thirteenth century and there are claims that it is of prehistoric origin.

Exmoor was largely ignored by the Roman conquerors. The local Dumnonii tribe, from whom Devon gets its name, seem to have been generally co-operative and the Romans were only interested in protecting the coast from raids by the warlike Silures of South Wales – hence the construction of the forts and signal stations at Old Barrow and Martinhoe Beacon. After the withdrawal of the Romans came the Saxon invaders, who slowly penetrated into the region via the river valleys from their chief base at Taunton. There is no clear evidence of the Saxon advance but by the early eighth century Exmoor and the Quantocks had been incorporated into the kingdom of Wessex. Viking activity, so prominent in many other parts of England, seems to have been confined here to a few sea battles in the Bristol Channel and raids on the ports of Watchet and Porlock.

Two particularly important dates stand out in the largely uneventful history of Exmoor and the first of these was 1066. The main impact of the Norman Conquest was the creation of a royal forest in the central heartland of the moor, an area in which the king had sole hunting rights that were protected and enforced by a harsh and rigid code of laws. There is, however, no record of medieval and later monarchs exercising those rights personally – compared with many of the other royal forests Exmoor was remote and there was no nearby royal castle or hunting lodge to use as a convenient base. But it was the creation of the royal forest, coupled with the climate and terrain, that preserved much of the wildness and openness of this part of Exmoor and prevented agricultural development; at the time of disafforestation in 1815 there were within the forest boundaries only one farm and one house, the former residence of the Warden of the Forest at Simonsbath, the 'forest capital'.

The second important date was 1818. In that year, following disafforestation, the Crown's allocation of the former forest lands was purchased by John Knight, a Worcestershire industrialist. He was a remarkable and energetic man

Nettlecombe – church and court side-by-side

whose main aim was to develop Exmoor as a profitable and successful agricultural community. Despite his efforts, and those of his son Sir Frederic, commercial success was never achieved, but the Knights did nevertheless reclaim many acres of barren moorland for farming and are largely responsible for much of Exmoor's present landscape pattern. They constructed roads, built farms, inaugurated drainage schemes, introduced crop growing and stock rearing and virtually created Simonsbath, the centre of their 'kingdom', building both the school and church there.

Other developments appeared around Exmoor's fringes during the nineteenth century. Wordsworth and Coleridge both lived for a brief time in the Quantocks — the former at Alfoxton, the latter at Nether Stowey — and although never popularising the area to the same extent as the Lake District, they did put it on the literary map. A later poet, Sir Henry Newbolt (of 'Play up! play up! and play the game!' fame) continued this literary tradition by often staying at the tiny Quantock hamlet of Aisholt, 'that beloved valley'.

More significant was the appearance of the first tourists on the scene in the early nineteenth century — mostly wealthy, aristocratic visitors who, cut off from their usual continental haunts by the Napoleonic Wars, were attracted to the area around Lynmouth and Lynton as a suitable alternative. It was not only the mild climate and picturesque situation that drew them there; they were also thrilled by such dramatic scenic wonders as the Valley of Rocks and the East Lyn and West Lyn gorges, comparing the latter favourably with Switzerland. Road improvements and the construction of railways later in the nineteenth century broke down much of the isolation of Exmoor for the first time and brought a much greater influx of tourists into the area, turning Minehead, Lynmouth, Lynton and Combe Martin into popular, though still relatively small and genteel, holiday resorts.

The twentieth century has brought many more tourists, as a result of the car and especially the construction of the M5, the planting of conifers, chiefly in the Brendon and Quantock forests, and the damming of the waters of the River Haddeo in the 1970s to create Wimbleball Lake. It has also brought demands for both conservation and recreation that have resulted in the acquisition of many of the most outstanding beauty spots by the National Trust, the creation of the Exmoor National Park in 1954 and the later designation of the Quantocks as an Area of Outstanding Natural Beauty.

Exmoor and the Quantocks comprise a relatively small area that includes a remarkable diversity of scenery. Its uniquely beautiful combination of moor and coast, woodland and valleys, hills and forest, wildness and gentleness, and openness and intimacy, makes it ideal for exploring on foot. Whatever your needs – be it a gentle half-day stroll or a longer and more energetic trek across hills and moors – Exmoor and the Quantocks can supply it, and wherever you are, spectacular and unspoilt views can be absolutely guaranteed.

View over Exmoor from Selworthy Beacon

The National Parks and countryside recreation

Ten National Parks were created in England and Wales as a result of an Act of Parliament in 1949. In addition to these, there are numerous specially designated Areas of Outstanding Natural Beauty, Country and Regional Parks, Sites of Special Scientific Interest and picnic areas scattered throughout England, Wales and Scotland, all of which share the twin aims of preservation of the countryside and public accessibility and enjoyment.

In trying to define a National Park, one point to bear in mind is that unlike many overseas ones, Britain's National Parks are not owned by the nation. The vast bulk of the land in them is under private ownership. John Dower, whose report in 1945 created their framework, defined a National Park as 'an extensive area of beautiful and relatively wild country in which, for the nation's benefit and by appropriate national decision and action, (a) the characteristic landscape beauty is strictly preserved, (b) access and facilities for public open-air enjoyment are amply provided, (c) wildlife and buildings and places of architectural and historic interest are suitably protected, while (d) established farming use is effectively maintained'.

The concept of having designated areas of protected countryside grew out of a number of factors that appeared towards the end of the nineteenth century; principally greater facilities and opportunities for travel, the development of various conservationist bodies and the establishment of National Parks abroad. Apart from a few of the early individual travellers such as Celia Fiennes and Daniel Defoe, who were usually more concerned with commenting on agricultural improvements, the appearance of towns and the extent of antiquities to be found than with the wonders of nature, interest in the countryside as a source of beauty, spiritual refreshment and recreation, and, along with that, an interest in conserving it, did not arise until the Victorian era. Towards the end of the eighteenth century, improvements in road transport enabled the wealthy to visit regions that had hitherto been largely inaccessible and, by the middle of the nineteenth century, the construction of the railways opened up such possibilities to the middle classes and, later on, to the working classes in even greater numbers. At the same time, the Romantic movement was in full swing and, encouraged by the works of Wordsworth, Coleridge and Shelley, interest and enthusiasm for wild places, including the mountain, moorland and hill regions of northern and western Britain, were now in vogue. Eighteenth-century taste had thought of the Scottish Highlands, the Lake District and Snowdonia as places to avoid, preferring controlled order and symmetry in nature as well as in architecture and town planning. But upper and middle class Victorian travellers were thrilled and awed by what they saw as the untamed savagery and wilderness of mountain peaks, deep and secluded gorges, thundering waterfalls, towering cliffs and rocky crags. In addition, there was a growing reaction against the materialism and squalor of Victorian industrialisation and urbanisation and a desire to escape from the formality and artificiality of town life into areas of unspoilt natural beauty.

A result of this was the formation of a number of different societies, all concerned with the 'great outdoors': naturalist groups, rambling clubs and conservationist organisations. One of the earliest of these was the Commons, Open Spaces and Footpaths Preservation Society, originally founded in 1865 to preserve commons and develop public access to the countryside. Particularly influential was the National Trust, set up in 1895 to protect and maintain both places of natural beauty and places of historic interest, and, later on, the Councils for the Preservation of Rural England, Wales and Scotland, three separate bodies that came into being between 1926 and 1928.

The world's first National Park was the Yellowstone Park in the United States, designated in 1872. This was followed by others in Canada, South Africa, Germany, Switzerland, New Zealand and elsewhere, but in Britain such places did not come about until after the Second World War. Proposals for the creation of areas of protected countryside were made before the First World War and during the 1920s and 1930s, but nothing was done. The growing demand from people in towns for access to open country and the reluctance of landowners — particularly

Combe Martin from Knap Down

those who owned large expanses of uncultivated moorland — to grant it led to a number of ugly incidents, in particular the mass trespass in the Peak District in 1932, when fighting took place between ramblers and game-keepers and some of the trespassers received stiff prison sentences.

It was in the climate exemplified by the Beveridge Report and the subsequent creation of the welfare state, however, that calls for country-side conservation and access came to fruition in parliament. Based on the recommendations of the Dower Report (1945) and the Hobhouse Committee (1947), the National Parks and Country-side Act of 1949 provided for the designation and preservation of areas both of great scenic beauty and of particular wildlife and scientific interest throughout Britain. More specifically it provided for the creation of National Parks in England and Wales. Scotland was excluded because, with greater areas of open space and a smaller population, there were fewer pressures on the Scottish countryside and there-fore there was felt to be less need for the creation of such protected areas.

A National Parks Commission was set up, and over the next eight years ten areas were designated as parks; seven in England (Northumberland, Lake District, North York Moors, Yorkshire Dales, Peak District, Exmoor and Dartmoor) and three in Wales (Snowdonia, Brecon Beacons and Pembrokeshire Coast). At the same time the Commission was also given the responsibility for designating other smaller areas of high recreational and scenic qualities (Areas of Outstanding Natural Beauty), plus the power to propose and develop long-distance footpaths, now called National Trails, though it was not until 1965 that the first of these, the Pennine Way, came into existence.

Further changes came with the Countryside Act of 1968 (a similar one for Scotland had been passed in 1967). The National Parks Commission was replaced by the Countryside Commis-sion, which was now to oversee and review virtually all aspects of country-side conservation, access and provision of recreational amenities. The Country Parks, which were smaller areas of countryside often close to urban areas, came into being. A number of long-distance footpaths were created, followed by an even greater number of unofficial long- or middle-distance paths, devised by individuals, ramblers' groups or local authorities. Provision of car parks and visitor centres, way-marking of public rights of way and the production of leaflets giving suggestions for walking routes all increased, a reflection both of increased leisure and of a greater desire for recreational activity, of which walking in particular, now recognised as the most popular leisure pursuit, has had a great explosion of interest.

The authorities who administer the individual National Parks have the very difficult task of reconciling the interests of the people who live and earn their living within them with those of the visitors. National Parks, and the other designated areas, are not living museums. Developments of various kinds, in housing, transport and rural industries, are needed. There is pressure to exploit the resources of the area, through more intensive farming, or through increased quarrying and forestry, extraction of minerals or the construction of reservoirs.

In the end it all comes down to a question of balance; a balance between conservation and 'sensitive develop-ment'. On the one hand there is a responsibility to preserve and enhance the natural beauty of the National Parks and to promote their enjoyment by the public, and on the other, the needs and well-being of the people living and working in them have to be borne in mind.

Thatched inn at West Bagborough, below the wooded slopes of the Quantocks

Quantock's Head dominates the coast near Kilve

The National Trust

Anyone who likes visiting places of natural beauty and/or historic interest has cause to be grateful to the National Trust. Without it, many such places would probably have vanished by now, either under an avalanche of concrete and bricks and mortar or through reservoir construction or blanket afforestation.

It was in response to the pressures on the countryside posed by the relentless march of Victorian industrialisation that the Trust was set up in 1895. Its founders, inspired by the common goals of protecting and conserving Britain's national heritage and widening public access to it, were Sir Robert Hunter, Octavia Hill and Canon Rawnsley; a solicitor, a social reformer and a clergyman respectively. The latter was particularly influential. As a canon of Carlisle Cathedral and vicar of Crosthwaite (near Keswick), he was concerned about threats to the Lake District and had already been active in protecting footpaths and promoting public access to open countryside. After the flooding of Thirlmere in 1879 to create a large reservoir, he and his two colleagues became increasingly convinced that the only effective protection was outright ownership of land.

The purpose of the National Trust is to preserve areas of natural beauty and sites of historic interest by acquisition, holding them in trust for the nation and making them available for public access and enjoyment. Some of its properties have been acquired through purchase, but many have been donated. Nowadays it is one of the biggest landowners in the country and protects over half a million acres of land, including nearly 500 miles of coastline and a large number of historic properties (mostly houses) in England, Wales and Northern Ireland. (There is a separate National Trust for Scotland, which was set up in 1931.)

Furthermore, once a piece of land has come under Trust ownership, it is difficult for its status to be altered. As a result of Parliamentary legislation in 1907, the Trust was given the right to declare its property inalienable, so ensuring that in any dispute it can appeal directly to Parliament.

As it works towards its dual aims of conserving areas of attractive countryside and encouraging greater public access (not easy to reconcile in this age of mass tourism), the Trust provides an excellent service to walkers by creating new concessionary paths and waymarked trails, by maintaining stiles and footbridges and by combating the ever increasing problem of footpath erosion.

The Ramblers' Association

No organisation works more actively to protect and extend the rights and interests of walkers in the countryside than the Ramblers' Association. Its aims (summarised here) are clear: to foster a greater knowledge, love and care of the countryside; to assist in the protection and enhancement of public rights of way and areas of natural beauty; to work for greater public access to the countryside and to encourage more people to take up rambling as a healthy, recreational activity.

It was founded in 1935 when, following the setting up of a National Council of Ramblers' Federation in 1931, a number of federations earlier formed in London, Manchester, the Midlands and elsewhere came together to create a more effective pressure group, to deal with such contemporary problems as the disappearance and obstruction of footpaths, the prevention of access to open mountain and moorland and increasing hostility from landowners. This was the era of the mass trespasses, when there were sometimes violent confrontations between ramblers and gamekeepers, especially on the moorlands of the Peak District.

Since then the Ramblers' Association has played an influential role in preserving and developing the national footpath network, supporting the creation of National Parks and encouraging the designation and way-marking of long-distance footpaths.

Our freedom to walk in the countryside is precarious, and requires constant vigilance. As well as the perennial problems of foot-paths being illegally obstructed, disappearing through lack of use or extinguished by housing or road construction, new dangers can spring up at any time.

It is to meet such problems and dangers that the Ramblers' Association exists and represents the interests of all walkers. The address to write to for information on the Ramblers' Association and how to become a member is given on page 78.

Walkers and the law

The average walker in a National Park or other popular walking area, armed with the appropriate Ordnance Survey map, rein-forced perhaps by a guidebook giving detailed walking instructions, is unlikely to run into legal difficulties, but it is useful to know something about the law relating to public rights of way. The right to walk over certain parts of the countryside has developed over a long period of time, and how such rights came into being and how far they are protected by the law is a complex subject, fascinating in its own right, but too lengthy to be discussed here. The following comments are intended simply to be a helpful guide, backed up by the Countryside Access Charter, a concise summary of walkers' rights and obligations drawn up by the Countryside Commission.

Basically there are two main kinds of public rights of way: footpaths (for walkers only) and bridle-ways (for walkers, riders on horseback and pedal cyclists). Footpaths and bridle-ways are shown by broken green lines on Ordnance Survey Pathfinder and Outdoor Leisure maps and broken red lines on Landranger maps. There is also a third category, called byways or 'roads used as a public path': chiefly broad, walled tracks (green lanes) or farm roads, which walkers, riders and cyclists have to share, usually only occasionally, with motor vehicles. Many of these public paths have been in existence for hundreds of years and some even originated as prehistoric trackways and have been in constant use for well over 2,000 years.

The term 'right of way' means exactly what it says. It gives right of passage over what, in the vast majority of cases, is private land, and you are required to keep to the line of the path and not stray onto the land either side. If you inadvertently wander off the right of way − either because of faulty map-reading or because the route is not clearly indicated on the ground − you are technically trespassing and the wisest course is to ask the nearest available person (farmer or fellow walker) to direct you back to the correct route. There are stories of unpleasant confrontations between walkers and farmers at times, but in general most farmers are helpful and co-operative when responding to a genuine and polite request for assistance in route finding.

Obstructions can sometimes be a problem and probably the commonest of these is where a path across a field has been ploughed up. It is legal for a farmer to plough up a path provided that he restores it within two weeks, barring exceptionally bad weather. This does not always happen and here the walker is presented with a dilemma. Does he follow the line of the path, even if this inevitably means treading on crops, or does he use his common sense and walk around the edge of the field? The latter course of action often seems the best but, as this means that you would be trespassing, you are, in law, supposed to keep to the exact line of the path, avoiding unnecessary damage to crops. In the case of other obstructions which may block a path (illegal fences and locked gates etc.), common sense again has to be used in order to negotiate them by the easiest method (detour or removal), followed by reporting the matter to the local council or National Park authority.

Apart from rights of way enshrined by law, there are a number of other paths available to walkers. Permissive or concessionary paths have been created where a landowner has given permission for the public to use a particular route across his land. The main problem with these is that, as they have been granted as a concession, there is no legal right to use them and therefore they can be extinguished at any time. In practice, many of these concessionary routes have been established on land owned either by large public bodies such as the Forestry Commission or the water authorities, or by a private one, such as the National Trust, and as these mainly encourage walkers to use their paths, they are unlikely to be closed unless a change of ownership occurs.

Walkers also have free access to Country Parks (except where requested to keep away from certain areas for ecological reasons e.g. wildlife protection, woodland regeneration, safeguarding of rare plants etc.), canal towpaths and most beaches. By custom, though not by right, you are generally free to walk across the open and uncultivated higher land of mountain, moorland and fell, but this varies from area to area and from one season to another — grouse moors, for example, will be out of bounds during the breeding and shooting seasons and some open areas are used as Ministry of Defence firing ranges, for which reason access will be restricted. In some areas the situation has been clarified as a result of 'access agreements' between the landowners and either the county council or the National Park authority, which clearly define when and where you can walk over such open country.

Countryside Access Charter

Your rights of way are:
- Public footpaths — on foot only. Sometimes waymarked in yellow
- Bridle-ways — on foot, horseback and pedal cycle. Sometimes waymarked in blue
- Byways (usually old roads), most 'roads used as public paths' and, of course, public roads — all traffic has the right of way.

Use maps, signs and waymarks to check rights of way. Ordnance Survey Pathfinder and Landranger maps show most public rights of way

On rights of way you can:
- take a pram, pushchair or wheelchair if practicable
- take a dog (on a lead or under close control)
- take a short route round an illegal obstruction or remove it sufficiently to get past

Harbour at Porlock

You have a right to go for recreation to:
- public parks and open spaces — on foot
- most commons near older towns and cities — on foot and sometimes on horseback
- private land where the owner has a formal agreement with the local authority

In addition you can use the following by local or established custom or consent, but ask for advice if you are unsure:
- many areas of open country, such as moorland, fell and coastal areas, especially those in the care of the National Trust, and some commons
- some woods and forests, especially those owned by the Forestry Commission
- Country Parks and picnic sites
- most beaches
- canal towpaths
- some private paths and tracks

Consent sometimes extends to horse-riding and cycling

For your information:
- county councils and London boroughs maintain and record rights of way, and register commons
- obstructions, dangerous animals, harassment and misleading signs on rights of way are illegal and you should report them to the county council
- paths across fields can be ploughed, but must normally be reinstated within two weeks
- landowners can require you to leave land to which you have no right of access
- motor vehicles are normally permitted only on roads, byways and some 'roads used as public paths'

Key Map

CONVENTIONAL SIGNS
1:25 000 or 2½ INCHES to 1 MILE

ROADS AND PATHS

Not necessarily rights of way

M I or A 6(M)	M I or A 6(M)	Motorway
A 31 (T)	A 31(T)	Trunk road
A 35	A 35	Main road
B 3074	B 3074	Secondary road
A 35	A 35	Dual carriageway

Narrow roads with passing places are annotated

Road generally more than 4m wide

Road generally less than 4m wide

Other road, drive or track

Unfenced roads and tracks are shown by pecked lines

Path

RAILWAYS

Multiple track	Standard gauge
Single track	
Narrow gauge	
Siding	
Cutting	
Embankment	
Tunnel	
Road over & under	
Level crossing; station	

PUBLIC RIGHTS OF WAY

Public rights of way may not be evident on the ground

Public paths { Footpath / Bridleway

+ + + + + Byway open to all traffic
-+-+-+-+- Road used as a public path

DANGER AREA

Firing and test ranges in the area
Danger!
Observe warning notices

The indication of a towpath in this book does not necessarily imply a public right of way
The representation of any other road, track or path is no evidence of the existence of a right of way

BOUNDARIES

— · — · — · — County (England and Wales)
— — — — — District
—·—·—·—·— London Borough
· · · · · · · · · · · · · · Civil Parish (England)* Community (Wales)
— — — — — — Constituency (County, Borough, Burgh or European Assembly)

Coincident boundaries are shown by the first appropriate symbol

*For Ordnance Survey purposes County Boundary is deemed to be the limit of the parish structure whether or not a parish area adjoins

SYMBOLS

♦	Place	with tower
♠	of	with spire, minaret or dome
+	worship	without such additions

☒ △ Glasshouse; youth hostel
⊖ Bus or coach station
Lighthouse; lightship; beacon
△ Triangulation station

Triangulation point on { church or chapel / lighthouse, beacon / building; chimney

pylon pole Electricity transmission line

VILLA Roman antiquity (AD 43 to AD 420)
Castle Other antiquities
Site of antiquity
1066 Site of battle (with date)
Gravel pit
Sand pit
Chalk pit, clay pit or quarry
Refuse or slag heap
Sloping wall

Water   Mud

Sand; sand & shingle

National Park or Forest Park Boundary

NT National Trust open access

NT National Trust limited access

NTS NTS National Trust for Scotland

VEGETATION

Limits of vegetation are defined by positioning of the symbols but may be delineated also by pecks or dots

Coniferous trees
Non-coniferous trees
Coppice

Orchard
Scrub
Marsh, reeds, saltings

Bracken, rough grassland
In some areas bracken ( ) and rough grassland ( ) are shown separately
Heath

Shown collectively as rough grassland on some sheets

In some areas reeds ( ) and saltings ( ) are shown separately

HEIGHTS AND ROCK FEATURES

50 ·   Determined { ground survey
285   by   { air survey

Surface heights are to the nearest metre above mean sea level. Heights shown close to a triangulation pillar refer to the ground level height at the pillar and not necessarily the summit.

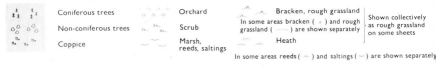

Vertical face

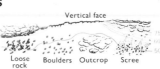

Loose rock   Boulders   Outcrop   Scree

Contours are at 5 metres vertical interval

TOURIST INFORMATION

♰	Abbey, Cathedral, Priory	❈	Garden	☆	Other tourist feature
🐟	Aquarium	▶	Golf course or links	✕	Picnic site
⋏	Camp site	🏛	Historic house	🚂	Preserved railway
🚐	Caravan site	ℹ	Information centre	🏃	Racecourse
🏰	Castle	⚙	Motor racing	⛷	Skiing
🕳	Cave	🏛	Museum	❄	Viewpoint
🏕	Country park	❗	Nature or forest trail	♈	Wildlife park
⚲	Craft centre	🐦	Nature reserve	🐘	Zoo
P	Parking				
PC	Public Convenience (in rural areas)	𝓒𝓪𝓼𝓽𝓵𝓮 SAILING	Selected places of interest		
		☎ T	Public telephone		
𝔐	Ancient Monuments and Historic Buildings in the care of the Secretary of State for the Environment which are open to the public.	⊕	Mountain rescue post		
◆	National trail or Recreational Path Long Distance Route (Scotland only)	NATIONAL PARK ACCESS LAND	Boundary of National Park access land Private land for which the National Park Planning Board have negotiated public access		
Pennine Way	Named path	◀	Access Point		

ABBREVIATIONS   1:25 000 or 2½ INCHES to 1 MILE also 1:10 000/1:10 560 or 6 INCHES to 1 MILE

BP,BS	Boundary Post or Stone	P	Post Office	A,R	Telephone, AA or RAC
CH	Club House	Pol Sta	Police Station	TH	Town Hall
F V	Ferry Foot or Vehicle	PC	Public Convenience	Twr	Tower
FB	Foot Bridge	PH	Public House	W	Well
HO	House	Sch	School	Wd Pp	Wind Pump
MP,MS	Mile Post or Stone	Spr	Spring		
Mon	Monument	T	Telephone, public		

Abbreviations applicable only to 1:10 000/1:10 560 or 6 INCHES to 1 MILE

Ch	Church	GP	Guide Post	TCB	Telephone Call Box
F Sta	Fire Station	P	Pole or Post	TCP	Telephone Call Post
Fn	Fountain	S	Stone	Y	Youth Hostel

WALKS

⚑1	Start point of walk		Featured walk	➤	Route of walk	▪▪❙▶▪ Alternative route

FOLLOW THE COUNTRY CODE
Enjoy the countryside and respect its life and work

Guard against all risk of fire

Fasten all gates

Keep your dogs under close control

Keep to public paths across farmland

Leave livestock, crops and machinery alone

Use gates and stiles to cross fences, hedges and walls

Take your litter home

Help to keep all water clean

Protect wildlife, plants and trees

Take special care on country roads

Make no unnecessary noise

Reproduced by permission of the Countryside Commission

1 East Quantoxhead and Kilve

Start:	Kilve Pill (on coast 1 mile (1.5 km) north of Kilve village)
Distance:	3 miles (4.75 km)
Approximate Time:	1 ½ hours
Parking:	Kilve Pill
Refreshments:	Pub at Kilve
Ordnance Survey maps:	Landranger 181 (Minehead & Brendon Hills area) and Pathfinder ST 04/14 1216 (Watchet)

General description *William and Dorothy Wordsworth, together with friend and fellow poet Coleridge, liked to walk beside 'Kilve's delightful shore', the attractive stretch of coast that lies below the abrupt northern edge of the Quantocks, during their stay at nearby Alfoxton. Within a remarkably short distance, this easy and very pleasant stroll embraces two splendid medieval churches, chapel ruins, an industrial relic and an enchanting village, plus fine views of coast, woodland and hills.*

Start by walking towards the shore, passing the 'Oil Retort House', the ruined building ahead that is the relic of an attempt in the 1920s to extract oil from local shale. Go through a gate, continue between trees, and on reaching the rocky shore **(A)** turn left along the low cliffs, passing through a gate. From here the all-round views are superb — to the right across the Bristol Channel to the coast of South Wales, ahead to the prominent headland of Quantock's Head and beyond that North Hill and the hills of Exmoor, and to the left the tower of Kilve church, in its tranquil setting about ½ mile (0.75 km) inland, backed by the slopes of the Quantock Hills.

Continue along the cliffs and just before reaching Quantock's Head turn left **(B)** along a broad grassy path between wire fences, heading inland — with a lovely view in front over a pleasant and gentle landscape of cornfields and wooded slopes — to go through a kissing-gate. Continue through another kissing-gate and in a few yards turn right, at a footpath sign to East Quantoxhead, along a track, by a stream on the right, into the village and up to a lane **(C)**.

East Quantoxhead is the quintessential English village: a place where time seems to have stood still. It has just about everything

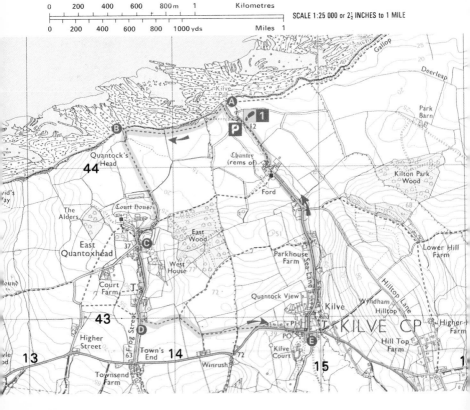

Church, house and village pond make a delightful composition at East Quantoxhead

except a village pub: old thatched cottages, duck-pond and an idyllic view across the pond to the church and great house standing side by side in the traditional manner. The house, the Court House, is a mainly seventeenth-century mansion owned by the Luttrell family, whose main residence for over seven centuries was nearby Dunster Castle. Inside the fourteenth-century church are tombs and monuments to the Luttrells.

Turn left along the lane and follow it for nearly ½ mile (0.75 km), turning left over a stile at a public footpath sign to Kilve (**D**). Continue, passing cottages on the left, across the middle of a field to climb a stile and turn half-right to head across the next field, looking out for a stile and public footpath sign at the far end. Climb over and continue across the next field to another stile, climb that and head across the next field, over one more stile and turn left along the main road into Kilve.

In the village centre turn left down Sea Lane (**E**) and follow it for 1 mile (1.5 km) back to the shore and car park, passing in turn Meadow House (with an attractive pond in front), Kilve church and the overgrown remains of a chantry chapel. Kilve's medieval church, a solid-looking but attractive building, occupies a lovely position between the Quantocks and the sea. The scanty ruins of the chantry chapel are a few yards further on, difficult to spot and impossible to make out any sort of plan. It is thought to have been destroyed around the middle of the nineteenth century because it was used as a contraband store by local smugglers, who were very active at that time along this stretch of the Somerset coast.

2 Hunter's Inn and Woody Bay

Start:	Hunter's Inn
Distance:	4 ½ miles (7.25 km)
Approximate Time:	2 ½ hours
Parking:	Hunter's Inn
Refreshments:	Hotel and café at Hunter's Inn
Ordnance Survey maps:	Landranger 180 (Barnstaple & Ilfracombe) and Pathfinder SS 64/74 1214 (Lynton & Lynmouth)

General description *Here is one of those ideal, leisurely, half-day walks which, with comparatively little effort, enables you to enjoy the most outstanding views. It divides itself naturally into three almost equal sections: above the lovely, steep-sided and thickly-wooded Heddon valley, the spectacular stretch of coast between Heddon's Mouth and Woody Bay, and along quiet paths and winding lanes back to the start at Hunter's Inn. The paths are generally wide and well surfaced with gentle gradients.*

Refer to map overleaf.

Even by Exmoor standards, the valley of the little River Heddon at Hunter's Inn is a particularly narrow, steep-sided and secluded one — accessible only by similarly narrow, steep and twisting lanes. Walk down the road towards Hunter's Inn and take the path to the right of it, signposted to Martinhoe, Woody Bay and Heddon's Mouth. Go through a gate to enter the National Trust property of Heddon Valley and, at a fork, take the upper path signposted Woody Bay through the splendid woodlands that clothe the steep sides of the Heddon valley. This broad, well surfaced path climbs gently above the valley, and on emerging from the trees there is a superb view to the left down the valley towards the coast at Heddon's Mouth. The path bears right and then left to cross the head of the valley of Hill Brook (**A**) and continues, still climbing steadily and curving right onto the cliffs above the Bristol Channel.

Keep along the cliffs for the next 1 ½ miles (2.5 km) — a superb coastal walk with fine views ahead looking towards Woody Bay, and beyond that to Lee Bay. Although a winding path, it is unusually wide, flat and well surfaced for a coastal footpath as it used to be an old coach road between Hunter's Inn and Woody Bay — a ride in a carriage along it with a sheer drop on one side to the rocks

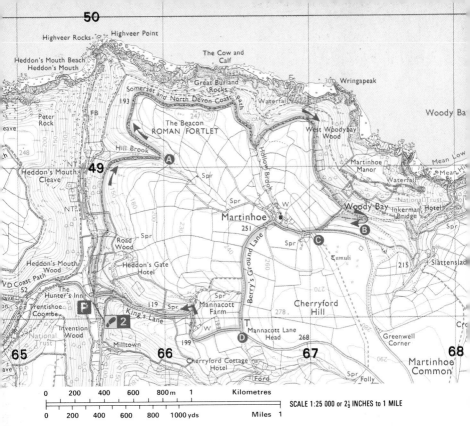

Highveer Rocks   Highveer Point

Heddon's Mouth Beach
Heddon's Mouth

The Cow and
Calf

Great Burland
Rocks

eave

Somerset and North Devon Coast Path

Waterfall

Wringapeak

Peter
Rock   FB   193

The Beacon
ROMAN FORTLET

West Woodybay
Wood

Woody Ba

Hill Brook

49

NT

Heddon's Mouth
Cleave

248

Martinhoe
Manor

Mean Low

Waterfall

NT

Spr

Spr

Spr

Woody Bay

Inkerman
Bridge

Hotel

B

Mean L

National
Trust

Road
Wood

Martinhoe
251

Spr

C

Spr

Spr

Tumuli

215

Slattenslad

Heddon's Mouth
Wood

Heddon's Gate
Hotel

Cr

Cherryford
Hill

Greenwell
Corner

Martinhoe
Common

VD Coast Path
52

The
Hunter's Inn

Trentishoe
Coombe

F

119

Spr

2

King's Lane

Mannacott
Farm

278

Berry's Ground Lane

Mannacott Lane
Head 268

Folly

Invention
Wood

Milltown

199

W

D

65   **66**   **67**   **68**

Cherryford Cottage
Hotel

Ford

A

```
0     200    400    600    800m    1          Kilometres
0     200    400    600    800  1000 yds       Miles  1
```

SCALE 1:25 000 or 2½ INCHES to 1 MILE

below must have been a somewhat nail-biting ordeal. After about 1 mile (1.5 km) go through a gate and continue along the top edge of West Woody Bay Wood; from here the views through the trees to the left across the bay are particularly memorable. Go through another gate at the end of the woods to come out onto a lane at a bend **(B)**.

Immediately turn sharp right, almost doubling back, along a narrow uphill bracken-lined path which later curves left and continues uphill, between banks, to emerge onto a lane **(C)**. Turn right through the hamlet of Martinhoe, passing its sturdy, plain thirteenth-century church on the right, after which the lane curves left and continues for ½ mile (0.75 km) to a T-junction **(D)**. Here turn right and follow another lane for just over ½ mile (0.75 km) as it curves first sharp right and then sharp left and continues steeply downhill through woodland back to Hunter's Inn.

Woody Bay from the coast path

3 Dulverton

Start:	Dulverton
Distance:	4 miles (6.5 km)
Approximate Time:	2 hours
Parking:	Dulverton
Refreshments:	Pubs and cafés at Dulverton
Ordnance Survey maps:	Landranger 181 (Minehead & Brendon Hills area) and Pathfinder SS 82/92 1256 (Dulverton)

General description *In its lower reaches the River Barle winds through a steep-sided, wooded valley just to the north of Dulverton, the last place it flows through before its confluence with the Exe, 2 miles (3.25 km) further downstream. This short walk explores part of this valley and serves as a modest, but nevertheless comprehensive, appetiser for the many delights of Exmoor: sparkling*

rivers, lovely woodlands, open moorlands and memorable views. The path through the riverside woods dips up and down almost continuously; apart from that there is one main ascent, fairly lengthy but not steep.

The thirteenth-century tower of the handsome and imposing church presides over the bright and bustling little town of Dulverton, the southern gateway to Exmoor, encircled by steep wooded hills. Near the fine old bridge over the Barle is a large, gracious-looking house that is the headquarters of the Exmoor National Park, its information centre full of useful and interesting books and leaflets on Exmoor.

Start by walking down to the bridge; cross it and turn right, at a footpath sign to Beech Tree Cross, Hawkridge and Tarr Steps, along a lane which heads uphill and continues as an enclosed track which climbs up to a footpath sign **(A)**. Keep ahead here (following directions to Tarr Steps and Hawkridge) along the edge of Burridge Wood for an extremely attractive walk by the Barle,

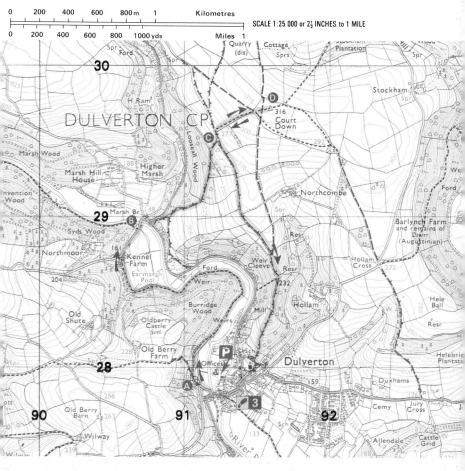

imes above and sometimes beside the river, for nearly 1½ miles (2.5 km). Eventually you pass through a gate and on to a lane. Continue along the lane to cross the Barle at Marsh Bridge (**B**), immediately turn right to cross a footbridge over a tributary stream and continue over the road and along the uphill lane ahead. At a T-junction keep ahead, at a footpath sign to Court Down, along an uphill track through Looseall Wood, climbing steadily and bearing left at the top to join another track (**C**).

Here make a detour to the viewpoint of Court Down by going through a metal gate in front. Keep ahead a few yards and then turn right off the track along the edge of a field, by a hedge-bank on the right, climbing gently over the down. Go through a gate on the right, at a gap in the hedge-bank, and continue straight ahead to the triangulation pillar on top of Court Down, a height of 1,036 ft (316 m) (**D**). From here there is a superb all-round view that includes the well-known landmarks of Anstey Common, Winsford Hill and Dunkery Beacon, and when clear the edge of Dartmoor can be seen across the farmlands of mid-Devon.

Return to the track just above Looseall Wood, turn left on to it and go through the metal gate (**C**). Continue along the track, first along the top edge of the wood, later gradually descending between hedge-banks, and finally veering slightly right and descending more steeply through woodland. Turn left just above Dulverton church and turn right down some steps, continuing past the church to the road. Keep ahead through the town back to the river.

Dulverton

4 Porlock Weir and Culbone

Start:	Porlock Weir
Distance:	5 miles (8 km)
Approximate Time:	2½ hours
Parking:	Porlock Weir
Refreshments:	Pubs and cafés at Porlock Weir
Ordnance Survey maps:	Landranger 181 (Minehead & Brendon Hills area) and Pathfinder SS 84/94 1215 (Minehead)

General description *From the small harbour of Porlock Weir the route proceeds through woodlands above the Bristol Channel to the delightful Culbone church, which claims to be the smallest and is certainly one of the most remote churches in England, accessible only on foot. The route then continues across more open country before re-entering woodland for the return to Porlock Weir. The combination of woodland and coast is extremely attractive at all seasons of the year. Although there are quite a number of ascents and descents for such a modest distance, they are all comparatively easy ones.*

The quiet, charming coastal settlement of Porlock Weir, which grew up as a successor to Porlock when the sea retreated from there, looks out across flat, reclaimed land to the imposing promontory of Hurlstone Point on the other side of Porlock Bay. Start by walking through the village, past the small harbour, and turn left up a flight of steps, at a red-waymarked footpath sign to Culbone church and County Gate, to a stile. Climb over, turn right along the edge of a field, by hedges and a wire fence on the right, go through a gate and continue along the right-hand edge of the next field. At the end of that field keep ahead, by a hedge on the left, to pass through the left-hand and higher of two adjacent gates and continue along a tarmac lane (**A**), following it as it bends slightly right past Worthy Manor to a toll gate.

Here the lane turns left but you keep ahead (**B**) to pass through a white gate and under an arch, at a footpath sign to Culbone and County Gate, continuing along a delightful path that soon heads uphill through Yearnor Wood. Pass under two bridges, turn left up some steps and turn sharp right at a footpath sign to Culbone to continue climbing gently through these attractive coastal woods. The path later levels off and descends to the tiny, beautifully situated, remote Culbone church, set in its deep, sheltered, wooded combe

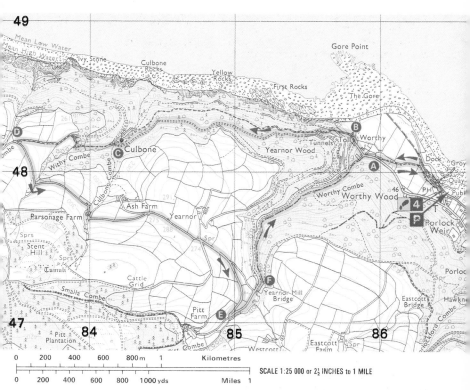

The delightful Culbone church claims to be the smallest and least accessible in England

400 ft (122 m) above the sea (C). Cross a footbridge over a stream and turn right to the church which is reputed to be the smallest complete parish church in England, only 35 ft (10.5 m) long and 12 ft (3.5 m) wide with a short, stumpy spire. Parts of it date back to the twelfth century. It once served a much more heavily populated parish than now: in the early nineteenth century the adjacent woods were inhabited by charcoal burners and a colony of lepers and there were cottages around the church and more farms in the vicinity.

Follow red-waymarked signs to County Gate and Silcombe through the churchyard, go through a gate at the far end and under the footbridge previously crossed, continuing uphill through the thick woodlands of Withy Combe on the right-hand side of the stream. Near the edge of the woods the path bends sharply right to a gate. Go through and keep climbing along the edge of the woods, turning left at a T-junction of paths to continue uphill between hedges. Go through two gates and keep ahead a few yards to a lane just above Silcombe Farm (D). Turn left along this narrow, winding, roller-coaster lane, from which there are superb views to the left over Porlock Bay, Hurlstone Point and beyond to the coast of South Wales, following it for 2 miles (3.25 km). Keep to the left at a fork and soon afterwards the lane

descends and turns sharp left, at a signpost to 'Porlock Weir via Worthy Toll Road' (E).

Continue downhill and near the bottom bear right (F) at a footpath sign to Porlock Weir and Porlock, to go through a gate into Worthy Wood. Cross a stream and just afterwards, where the track starts to ascend, turn sharp left (look out for blue waymarks on the trees) down a narrower, stony path and follow it through the delightful, wooded Worthy Combe, roughly parallel with and above the stream and toll road on the left. Continue gently downhill all the time, passing to the right of a cottage at one point and finally coming out onto a lane. Turn right and retrace your steps to Porlock Weir.

5 Lynton and Valley of Rocks

Start:	Lynton
Distance:	5 ½ miles (8.75 km)
Approximate Time:	2 ½ hours
Parking:	Lynton
Refreshments:	Pubs and cafés at Lynton
Ordnance Survey maps:	Landranger 180 (Barnstaple & Ilfracombe) and Pathfinder SS 64/74 1214 (Lynton & Lynmouth)

General description *This walk illustrates why Lynton has always been a favourite spot for those who appreciate fine coastal scenery. The first part is along a splendid path that leads westwards along the coast into the spectacular Valley of Rocks. The return to Lynton is through pleasant woodland, by a quiet combe and along a narrow winding lane — with outstanding views all the way — to conclude an exceptionally varied, attractive and, at the same time, easy walk.*

Lynton is the twin of Lynmouth, the former near the top of wooded Hollerday Hill and the latter at its base by the mouth of the East and West Lyn rivers. The two are linked by a steep road, even steeper paths and a cliff railway built in 1890. Both became fashionable resorts in the nineteenth century when a combination of outstanding scenery and a mild climate made them popular with affluent and discerning Victorian visitors. Lynton is a predominantly Victorian town, with a church and several large hotels from that period.

Begin in front of the church by turning down North Walk Hill, between the church and Valley of Rocks Hotel, at a public footpath sign to Valley of Rocks and Lynmouth. To the right is a fine view of the headland of The Foreland across the steep, wooded East Lyn valley. Following signs to North Walk and Valley of Rocks, continue over the bridge that crosses the cliff railway and along a pleasant tree-lined drive, passing in front of hotels. The drive later becomes a tarmac path which after emerging from the

0	200	400	600	800 m	1		Kilometres

SCALE 1:25 000 or 2½ INCHES to 1 MILE

0	200	400	600	800	1000 yds		Miles 1

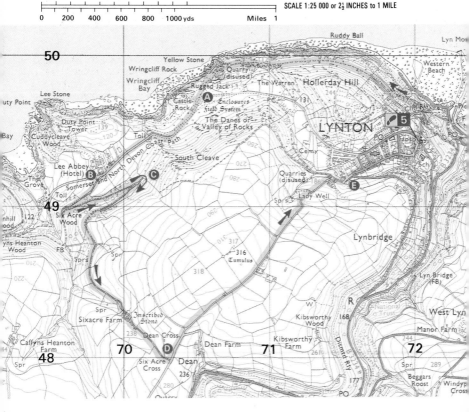

trees keeps above the sea, with grand views across to the South Wales coast. At a path junction continue ahead, the route signposted 'Lynton via Valley of Rocks', along this attractive, winding coastal path to reach the dramatic Valley of Rocks, the view dominated by the impressive Castle Rock immediately ahead. This rock-strewn valley, running parallel to the coast, has some interesting and spectacular rock formations, brought about by the action of the weather on a mixture of hard and soft rocks. These have been the favourite subject of artists, poets and photographers and the scene can sometimes be further enhanced by a glimpse of the wild goats that still roam through the valley.

Turn right on joining a lane **(A)** (this is a private toll road through the Lee Abbey Estate but only motorists pay the toll) and follow it for just over ½ mile (0.75 km) to Lee Abbey, which is neither a church nor a pile of ruins but a large Gothic house built in the nineteenth century. Here the lane bears right down to the coast at Lee Bay but you bear left **(B)**, at a footpath sign to 'Lynton over Southcliffe', through a gate and along a track. The track enters Six Acre Wood and curves left to a path junction. Here turn sharp left, almost doubling back, following both a bridle-path sign to Six Acre Cross and a footpath sign 'Lynton via Southcliffe'. The path continues through the wood, climbing gently and giving fine views to the left over Lee Abbey to the Castle Rock beyond. At a public bridle-way sign to Six Acre Cross and Lynton turn sharp right **(C)**, again almost doubling back, along a path which continues uphill through the wood, eventually bearing left to a gate. Go through and keep ahead into more open country of grassland and bracken, above a pleasant wooded valley on the right, later continuing, between a hedge-bank on the left and a wall on the right, through gates to Sixacre Farm. After passing the farm on the right the path becomes a tarmac drive which continues to a lane at Six Acre Cross **(D)**.

Turn left and at a signpost which says 'Lynton – Unfit for Motors' continue ahead along the narrow lane for 1 mile (1.5 km) back to Lynton. All the way along there are spectacular views: at first to the right over wooded valleys and fields to open moorland on the horizon, and later some fine coastal views ahead looking towards Hollerday Hill and The Foreland – Lynton and Lynmouth occupying the gap between them – and beyond to the South Wales coast. The lane drops steeply into Lynton, curves right at a footpath sign and then left down to a road **(E)**. Keep ahead along the road back to Lynton church, its tower a prominent landmark.

Start:	Minehead
Distance:	5 miles (8 km)
Approximate Time:	2 ½ hours
Parking:	Minehead
Refreshments:	Restaurants, pubs and cafés at Minehead
Ordnance Survey maps:	Landranger 181 (Minehead & Brendon Hills area) and Pathfinder SS 84/94 1215 (Minehead)

General description Geographically and scenically North Hill serves as an introduction to the Exmoor coast. It rises abruptly above Minehead on the eastern fringe of the National Park and marks the start of a succession of spectacular hog's-backed cliffs that stretch almost uninterruptedly, apart from the Vale of Porlock, to Combe Martin on the western edge and beyond. Its pine-clad, heather and bracken covered slopes provide the walker with a fine sample of what this stretch of coast can offer, with magnificent views both over the Bristol Channel and inland over the Quantocks, Brendons and Exmoor. After an initial lengthy zigzag climb the route levels off and the return to Minehead is almost all downhill.

Refer to map overleaf.

Away from the ornamental gardens, hotels, shops and cafés of the popular and well laid-out holiday resort, there is another Minehead – quieter and older, dating from its days as a fishing and cloth exporting port. Leading to the small harbour is a row of attractive fishermen's cottages and above it, in Higher Town, are steep streets and cobbled alleys, lined with attractive old houses that lead up to the handsome, late medieval church. Like the one at nearby Dunster, this is noted for its fine Perpendicular tower and fifteenth-century rood screen.

The walk starts in Quay Street, just before the harbour, where you turn onto a path at a sign 'Path to North Hill'; on the other side of the road another sign reveals that this marks the start of the rather more ambitious 500-mile South West Coast Footpath to Poole. The first part of the walk is a zigzag route that climbs by a series of steps through the lovely pine woods that clothe the slopes of North Hill, following coast path signs and acorn symbols – a most attractive beginning with plenty of seats and benches on which to take a rest. On reaching a lane turn sharp right, here parting company with the coast path to continue along a path on the left-hand side of the lane, still zigzagging upwards through the

North Hill, rising abruptly from Minehead harbour, marks the start of Exmoor's coast

woods. Keep along the higher path at any junctions and bear right on joining a wider path, at a footpath sign to Selworthy Beacon. At the next fork, immediately in front, continue along the left-hand path through the beautiful Culver Cliff Woods, along a path which levels out and then climbs more gently. Take the right-hand path at the next fork, soon leaving the woods, and continue across bracken, gorse, heather and random trees, with fine views over the sea to the right across to South Wales, up to a path junction and footpath sign (**A**).

To the right a path leads down into the steep Burgundy Combe, with its scanty remains of a chapel, but you continue by turning left, at a footpath sign to Woodcombe, to a road. Turn right along the road for 150 yards (138 m) and at another sign to Woodcombe turn left along a path that heads downhill across heathery moorland, bearing left into the pleasantly sylvan Wood Combe. Turn uphill along the first path on the left and after 50 yards (46 m) bear right along a level path that winds along the left-hand side of the steep-sided combe, later bearing left where the combe opens out into the main valley. Here the views are magnificent: Minehead below, the thickly wooded slopes of the Brendons ahead, Dunster Castle on its abrupt wooded hill, the line of the Quantocks to the left, and Dunkery Beacon and beyond it moorlands to the right. As the path continues to bear left another excellent view opens up ahead: along the flatter coastlands towards the Quantock ridge on the horizon.

At a path junction (**B**) turn right downhill, curving left through trees to a road (**C**). Turn right to follow the road sharply to the left through a lovely avenue of trees, then sharp right into Higher Town, the old part of Minehead, passing the church, thatched cottages and picturesque Church Steps. Continue downhill and where the road turns sharp right at the war memorial keep ahead along a cul-de-sac. Then continue along the footpath ahead to descend, retracing your steps along the path which zigzags down to the harbour.

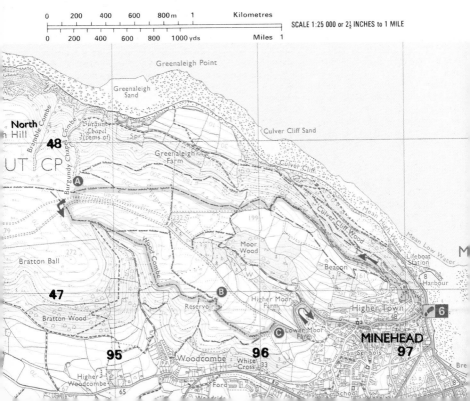

7 Dunster Park and Withycombe Hill

Start:	Dunster
Distance:	5½ miles (8.75 km)
Approximate Time:	2½ hours
Parking:	Gallox Bridge, Dunster
Refreshments:	Pubs and cafés at Dunster, pub at Carhampton
Ordnance Survey maps:	Landranger 181 (Minehead & Brendon Hills area), Pathfinders SS 84/94 1215 (Minehead) and ST 04/14 1216 (Watchet)

General description *The first and last parts of this pleasant and undemanding walk are within the boundaries of the former deer park that adjoins Dunster Castle, the middle section extending beyond the park to include the villages of Carhampton and Withycombe and a climb over Withycombe Hill. There are extensive views over Exmoor, the Brendons and the Quantocks, some attractive wooded stretches, and the walk is short enough to leave plenty of time to explore the town of Dunster, a most rewarding experience.*

Refer to map overleaf.

It is not surprising that the little town of Dunster is so popular: virtually every view of it and from it is photogenic. It is pleasantly situated on the River Avill, close to the coast and encircled on three sides by wooded hills, and it has a splendid assortment of attractive and interesting buildings and an extensive selection of hotels and restaurants, inns and tea shops. What is surprising is that it was once a port, as it is a mile (1.5 km) from the sea and the river looks scarcely wide or deep enough to take toy boats.

The town grew up in the shadow of the great castle, originally built soon after the Norman Conquest and for 600 years in the possession of one family, the Luttrells, until given by them to the National Trust in 1976. Apart from the thirteenth-century gatehouse, most of the present castle is the result of extensive nineteenth-century rebuilding carried out for George Luttrell by the renowned Victorian architect Anthony Salvin, and its irregular towers and battlemented walls present a picturesque pile perched on their wooded hill. The interior is sumptuous and both the gardens, and the views from them, are splendid.

Almost rivalling the castle is the church, a cruciform building that is unusually large and imposing for such a small town. This is because it was once part of a Benedictine priory, founded in the twelfth century as a daughter house of Bath Abbey. Little remains of the Norman church apart from the west door; the present building dates mainly from the fifteenth century and is dominated by its fine 100 ft (30 m) high Perpendicular tower. Inside, the church is notable for its unusually wide rood screen and the monuments to the Luttrells. Other monastic remains include a tithe barn, two gateways and a dovecote. Dunster was an important cloth-making centre in the Middle Ages and later, and the much-photographed seventeenth-century Yarn Market in the High Street is the most visible reminder of this. Opposite is the Luttrell Arms, once the residence of the abbots of Cleeve, and nearby in Church Street is the 'Nunnery', an attractive, medieval, timber-framed house, three-storeys high and hung with slates.

Turn left out of the car park, cross the River Avill by Gallox Bridge, a picturesque medieval pack-horse bridge, and keep ahead to a footpath sign at the edge of woodland **(A)**. Here turn left, following signs to Withycombe and Carhampton, and climb a stile to follow a red-waymarked route through Dunster Park, formerly the deer park attached to the castle. At the next footpath sign keep ahead, following directions to Carhampton, along a gently undulating path across grass and bracken to a gate. To the left is a superb comprehensive view that takes in the castle, the town, the wooded line of Grabbist Hill, the prominent eighteenth-century folly of Conygar Tower on its thickly-wooded conical hill and the coast beyond. Go through the gate and at a public footpath sign to Carhampton continue climbing gently up to pass through another gate, Carhampton Gate, on the edge of the park

Dunster Castle perches on its wooded eminence above town and park

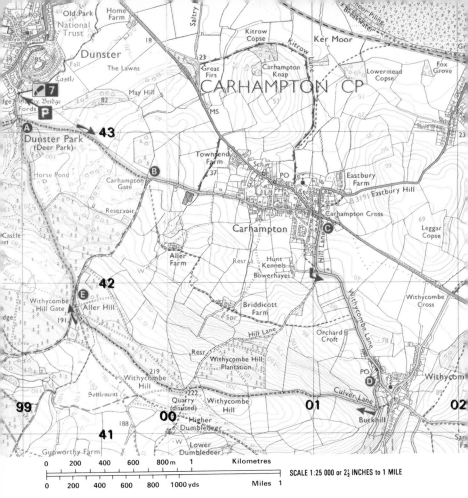

SCALE 1:25 000 or 2½ INCHES to 1 MILE

(B). Keep ahead down a tree-lined track — later a tarmac lane — which you follow for ¾ mile (1.25 km) into Carhampton, a large village which is a mixture of older thatched cottages and modern residential areas. The heavily restored medieval church has a rood screen almost as fine as that in Dunster Priory.

Continue to the main road, turn right along it for 100 yards (92 m) and take the first turning on the right **(C)**, signposted to Withycombe. Follow a narrow lane between hedge-banks for nearly 1 mile (1.5 km) into the unpretentious, tranquil little village of Withycombe, centred on its delightfully unspoilt, white-painted church. Inside it are two splendid medieval effigies, one male and one female.

Just before the church turn right **(D)**, at a public footpath sign 'Dunster via Withycombe Hill', along an uphill track that climbs quite steeply between trees, bearing right to a kissing-gate. Go through and continue climbing across gorse and open grassland, following a red-waymarked route over Withycombe Hill, from which there are

superb views to the right of the Quantocks, the Bristol Channel, Carhampton, Dunster Castle, Minehead and North Hill. Skirting Withycombe Plantation on the right, you come to a wire fence on the left which you follow to go through a gate. Now come more superb views — this time to the left looking towards the Brendon Hills. Pass through a gate, keep along the edge of Aller Hill Plantation on the right, go through another gate and continue through the plantation to a junction of tracks at Withycombe Hill Gate **(E)**.

Go through and bear right at a footpath sign to Dunster to re-enter Dunster Park, following red waymarks through dense conifer plantations. At first head gradually downhill, then turn right and continue more steeply downhill through a magnificent oak wood that lines both sides of the valley, with occasional glimpses of Dunster Castle ahead between the trees — an excellent finale. Finally go through a gate, bear left at the footpath sign ahead, climb a stile and turn right to retrace your steps over Gallox Bridge into Dunster.

8 Pittcombe Head and Robber's Bridge

Start:	Pittcombe Head
Distance:	4 miles (6.5 km)
Approximate Time:	2 hours
Parking:	National Park car park and picnic area at Pittcombe Head
Refreshments:	Culbone Inn
Ordnance Survey maps:	Landranger 181 (Minehead & Brendon Hills area) and Pathfinder SS 84/94 1215 (Minehead)

General description Starting high up on a ridge between the moors and the sea, the route descends in turn into the valleys on either side – Weir Water to the south and Smalla Combe to the north. The two descents are inevitably followed by two sharp climbs and so despite its modest length this is quite an energetic walk. It has fine views over both moorland and coast and some attractive wooded stretches.

Turn right out of the car park and walk along the main road in the Lynmouth direction for just over ¼ mile (0.5 km). Take the first turning on the left **(A)** and follow a pleasant winding lane downhill for 1 mile (1.5 km) into the lovely peaceful valley of Weir Water, ultimately joining the stream on the left and keeping by it to Robber's Bridge – a delightful, shady spot which has associations with the villainous exploits of the Doones, hence its name.

Do not cross the bridge but turn right **(B)** up to a red-waymarked footpath sign to 'Culbone Stables and A39 Road'. Here turn right along a path that heads uphill back along the side of the valley to a gate. Go through and continue, gradually curving left along the edge of the tributary valley of Met Combe and bearing right through an avenue of trees across the top of the combe to go through a gate. Continue up to the main road, passing to the right of the Culbone Inn **(C)**.

Cross over the road and take the lane opposite, at a footpath sign to Culbone, following it for nearly ½ mile (0.75 km). As it starts to descend there is a fine view ahead across the Bristol Channel to the coast of South Wales. Soon after the lane bears right; turn right **(D)**, at a footpath sign to Porlock Weir, along a track which heads downhill through Smalla Combe, over a stream – after which the path becomes increasingly narrow and the combe more wooded – and down to a footpath sign just above Pitt Farm. Here bear right, at a yellow-waymarked sign to Pittcombe Head, keeping to the right at a fork along the upper path and heading uphill along the edge of the conifer plantations of Pitt Combe. Keep bearing left all the while to cross the top of the combe – with superb views to the left of Porlock Bay, Hurlstone Point and Bossington Hill – and continue uphill, through a metal gate and back to the main road at Pittcombe Head.

SCALE 1:25 000 or 2½ INCHES to 1 MILE

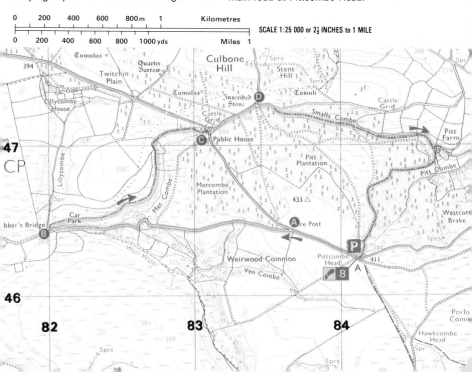

9 Roadwater and Nettlecombe

Start:	Roadwater
Distance:	5 miles (8 km)
Approximate Time:	2½ hours
Parking:	Roadside parking in Roadwater (either at places where the narrow road through the village widens or at the side of the 'Mineral Line' just after the start of the walk)
Refreshments:	Pub at Roadwater
Ordnance Survey maps:	Landranger 181 (Minehead & Brendon Hills area) and Pathfinder ST 03/13 (Quantock Hills)

General description *When walking in the Brendon Hills, on the eastern fringes of Exmoor, it is difficult to envisage this quiet, rural and sparsely populated backwater of deep wooded valleys and steep rolling hills as an important iron-mining area, which it was in the nineteenth century. A railway line was constructed to carry the ore from the mines down to the coast and this walk begins by following a section of this 'Mineral Line' along the narrow Roadwater valley. The walk continues through woodland and across fields to Nettlecombe before heading back over the hills to Roadwater. Apart from the disused line, there are few other signs of this former industrial activity on what is an extremely beautiful and fairly hilly walk.*

The walk starts in the centre of the small, pretty village of Roadwater which straggles along the narrow, steep-sided valley of the little Washford River. At a notice saying 'Road Ahead Narrows to 9' Width' turn down a lane between houses and cottages and take the first turning on the right (there are some parking spaces along here) to follow the course of the old 'Mineral Line', now a tarmac lane. The mining of iron ore in the Brendon Hills, which dates back to Roman times, reached its peak in the second half of the nineteenth century. Transport was a major problem and the West Somerset Mineral Railway was therefore built. A line linked the mines along the main ridge of the Brendons and a remarkable incline (¾ mile (1.25 km) long and with a gradient of 1 in 4) was constructed, by which the ore-laden wagons were lowered 800 ft (244 m) to the valley below at Comberow. Another line continued along the Washford valley to the

port of Watchet, from where the ore was shipped across to the furnaces of South Wales. By the end of the nineteenth century the mines had become uneconomic and they and the line closed down just before the First World War.

Keep along this now quiet and pleasant, tree-shaded lane for almost 1 mile (1.5 km) and just in front of a wire fence turn right (**A**). Cross a footbridge, passing a house on the right, and bear left uphill along a narrow enclosed path, then bearing right and again left. Turn right at a tarmac drive and continue between houses up to a lane where you turn left (**B**) passing Leighland Chapel, formerly belonging to nearby Cleeve Abbey and rebuilt in 1862 to serve the growing number of iron miners.

Continue downhill along a narrow lane, turning left between steep hedge-banks, then bearing right before Pitt Mill Farm and continuing to a public footpath sign. Turn sharp left down to the river, cross it and head up to rejoin the 'Mineral Line' (**C**). To the right the line continues as a woodland track to the base of the incline at Comberow but you keep ahead here, at a footpath sign to Chidgley, along a path that bears right through conifer plantations, at first running parallel to and above the 'Mineral Line' to the right but soon bearing sharply left and continuing uphill to a path junction and footpath sign. Turn sharp right, in the direction signposted Chidgley, and continue along a yellow-waymarked route through the plantation, still climbing gently. Go through a gate to emerge from the woods and continue along a very attractive path along the side of the valley by a line of trees on the left. To the right the views over the wooded slopes of the Brendon Hills are superb. Bear right to go through a metal gate and keep ahead, between a hedge on the left and a wire fence on the right, to go through another metal gate. Continue through Chidgley Farm and through another metal gate onto a road (**D**).

Turn left for just over ¼ mile (0.5 km) and at a footpath sign to Nettlecombe (**E**), climb a stile on the right and head down a grassy path – with a good view on the right across rolling country to the Quantocks – bearing right to follow the field edge down to a kissing-gate. Turn left through the gate and continue along the right hand edge of Kings Wood, following the yellow waymarks through a gate and on through Nettlecombe Park. Continue through two more gates and ahead there is an idyllic view of Nettlecombe, with the church and house side by side. Cross the field to a stile, climb over and pass to the right of the church (**F**), following the boundary of the churchyard round to the left up to the back of the house. Nettlecombe Court, basically a Tudor manor house with eighteenth-century additions (principally the west front), has been the home of two distinguished families: the Raleighs and later the Trevelyans. It is now a field study centre. The attractive thirteenth-century church standing next to it, comprehensively restored in the nineteenth century, has a fine tower and contains monuments to the Raleighs.

Turn right along a tarmac drive which first bends to the left, and where it curves right keep ahead through a gate and along a track for a few yards, and then bear left along a grassy path to another gate. Go through that and continue uphill, following a red-waymarked route along the left-hand edge of a field, to climb a stile in the top corner. Continue uphill through trees to climb another stile onto a road (G).

Cross over, go through a gate opposite at a footpath sign to Roadwater and continue along an uphill track, still a red-waymarked route. Where the track turns left, keep ahead along a path between hedges on the left and a wire fence on the right. To the right is an excellent view across sweeping fields of green and gold down to the flatter lands of the coast and sea beyond, bounded on the left by North Hill and Exmoor and on the right by the Quantocks. Climb a stile and continue

along the left-hand edge of a sloping field, over another stile and along the edge of the next field, turning right for a few yards at the end of that field and then turning left over a stile. Continue along the right-hand edge of the next field for another superb view ahead over the Roadwater valley and Brendon Hills to the coast and beyond to North Hill and Exmoor. Descend to pass through a gap in the hedge on the right, bear left and continue downhill across the middle of the next field, through a gap and onto a narrow lane (H).

Turn left down this lane for about 50 yards (46 m) and at a footpath sign turn right over a stile and along the left-hand edge of a field, following it as it curves left downhill to a stile. Climb over, continue along a narrow path between a hedge on the left and wire fence on the right to climb another stile and continue along the left-hand edge of a field, with a hedge and trees on the left, curving slightly left to a stile and footpath sign in the bottom corner. Climb the stile, turn right along the right-hand edge of the next field for a few yards, climb another stile on the right, turn left and continue through a wood, by a wire fence on the left, down to a stile. Climb over onto a lane (J) and turn right to follow it downhill for ¼ mile (0.5 km) into Roadwater.

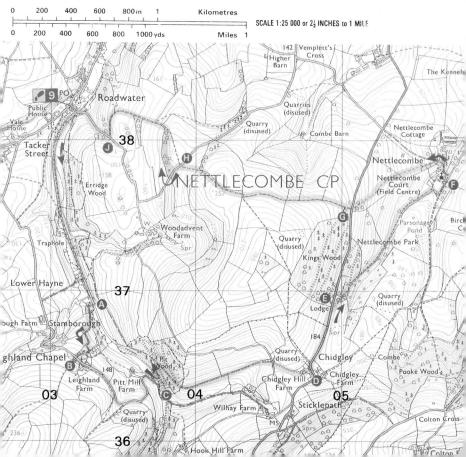

10 Wills Neck and Triscombe Combe

Start:	Lydeard Hill
Distance:	6 miles (9.5 km)
Approximate Time:	3 hours
Parking:	Lydeard Hill
Refreshments:	Pub at Triscombe, pub at West Bagborough
Ordnance Survey maps:	Landranger 181 (Minehead & Brendon Hills area) and Pathfinder ST 03/13 (Quantock Hills)

General description To the east of Exmoor rise the Quantocks, a compact range of hills about 12 miles (19 km) long and 3 miles (4.75 km) wide, stretching from just north of Taunton to the Bristol Channel. A superb path runs across the top of the ridge north-westwards from Lydeard Hill, passing Wills Neck, the highest point; the first part of the walk is along this path. The views from it over both sides reveal the English landscape at its very finest and most traditional – a lovely patchwork of fields, hedges and woods and a glorious riot of greens, golds and browns. After descending through Triscombe Combe, the walk continues across fields to the village of West Bagborough, sheltering beneath wooded slopes. The Quantock ridge is regained by the only climb on the walk, although it is a fairly steep one.

Go through a gate next to a stile at the far end of the car park and bear right along a broad track which heads gently up across the heathland of Lydeard Hill. At 1197 ft (364 m) this is the second highest point on the Quantocks and a superb 360-degree viewpoint: to the east over the Somerset Levels to the Mendips, to the north along the Quantock Ridge to Wills Neck, to the west across the valley to the Brendons and the hills of Exmoor in the distance, and to the south over the Vale of Taunton Deane to the Black Down Hills.

Now continue to the highest point on the Quantocks. Descend gently to the trees ahead (**A**), climb a stile (or go through a gate) and continue beside the woodlands of Bagborough Plantation on the left. Where the track forks keep ahead and climb gently across heather and gorse to the triangulation pillar on the summit of Wills Neck (1260 ft

SCALE 1:25 000 or 2½ INCHES to 1 MILE

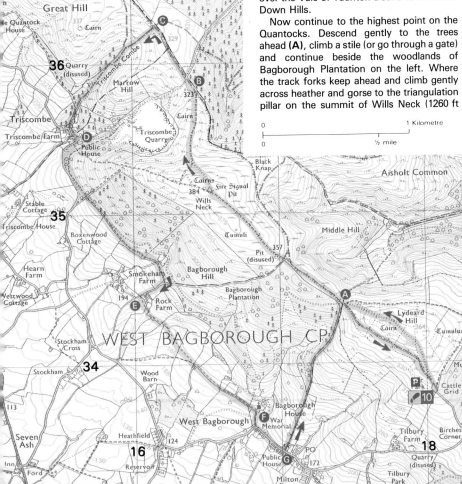

The magnificent view from Lydeard Hill – looking towards the Brendons and Exmoor

(384 m)), another magnificent all-round viewpoint – this time with the view to the north dominated by Great Hill.

At the triangulation pillar bear right along a track which descends gently, bears right towards the plantations of Quantock Forest and then bears left along the edge of those plantations for a few yards to the Triscombe Stone (**B**), an ancient stone around which all kinds of superstitious tales have been woven. From here continue through a delightful avenue of ancient and gnarled beeches, passing through a gate to enter the National Trust property of 'Great and Marrow Hills, Triscombe'. Shortly afterwards look out for a gap in the line of beeches on the left and turn left (**C**) to head downhill along a curving path through Triscombe Combe, sandwiched between Wills Neck on the left – its northern face eaten into by a large quarry, and Great Hill on the right. As you descend between bracken-covered slopes on the left and tree-covered slopes on the right, there are splendid views ahead of the Brendon Hills. On reaching the lane at the bottom bear left down to the road at the hamlet of Triscombe (**D**).

Turn left beside the thatched pub and then turn right at a signpost to Bagborough along a narrow, wooded uphill lane which curves gradually to the left. About 100 yards (92 m) before the lane bends to the right, bear slightly left along the right-hand one of two parallel paths, heading through trees to a gate. Pass through a gap in the hedge to the right of the gate and continue along the right-hand edge of a wood (there are several forks but keep by the edge of the wood all the time), finally bearing right downhill and passing Rock Farm on the left. Just past the farm look out for a kissing-gate in the hedge on the left (**E**).

Go through it and continue along the edge of a field, by a hedge on the left, following it round to the right to a gate. Turn left through the gate, keep ahead to climb a stile and follow the right-hand edge of the next field down to a metal gate. Go through it, and through another one a few yards ahead, and continue across the middle of the next field, from which there are fine views of the Black Down Hills ahead. Pass through another metal gate and continue to the far right-hand corner of the next field where you turn right through a gate. Immediately turn left through another one and keep ahead along the left-hand edge of a field, with a hedge on the left, passing through another gate and continuing along a grassy path enclosed by hedges to go through a gate into the churchyard of West Bagborough. The tranquil scene of church and hall standing side by side could hardly be more traditional. Neither building is particularly outstanding and they are separated in time by three centuries, but they are in perfect harmony with each other and with their surroundings on the edge of the village. The house is a dignified eighteenth-century building and the church is a typical parish church of the later Middle Ages, with a fine fifteenth-century tower.

Turn right by the south porch of the church, down the drive to the road (**F**) and turn left into the attractive village which lies below the south-western slopes of the Quantocks. By the side of the thatched pub (**G**) turn left by cottages along an uphill track to go through a gate. Now comes the only reasonably strenuous part of the walk: an unremitting climb of ¾ mile (1.25 km) along an enclosed track, later continuing by the right-hand edge of Bagborough Plantation to regain the Quantock ridge. On reaching the top (**A**) turn right, through either the stile or the gate, and return to the starting point either by retracing the outward route or following a parallel path which keeps by a wire fence on the right.

11 Little and Great Hangman

Start: Combe Martin

Distance: 5 miles (8 km)

Approximate Time: 3 hours

Parking: Kiln car park, near harbour at Combe Martin

Refreshments: Pubs and cafés at Combe Martin

Ordnance Survey maps: Landranger 180 (Barnstaple & Ilfracombe), Pathfinders SS 44/54 (and part of SS 14) 1213 (Ilfracombe & Lundy Island) and SS 64/74 1214 (Lynton & Lynmouth)

General description On the eastern side of Combe Martin Bay the abrupt cliff of Little Hangman rises to 716 ft (219 m). Immediately to the east of that, rising somewhat less abruptly to 1043 ft (318 m), is Great Hangman. The walk begins by climbing over this spectacular stretch of coast, then it heads inland over Girt Down and Knap Down to return to Combe Martin. Do not be deceived by this walk: although short, it is quite strenuous in parts – especially the initial ascent to Little Hangman. But the views from this majestic, rocky coastline, both along the coast itself and inland over Exmoor, are truly magnificent.

Combe Martin straggles for nearly 1½ miles (2.5 km) along a narrow combe which reaches down to a sheltered bay and harbour with a fine sandy beach, which make it a popular holiday resort. It used to be the centre of a small mining area (lead, silver, iron), and in the nineteenth century there was quite a substantial traffic in iron ore across

Little Hangman

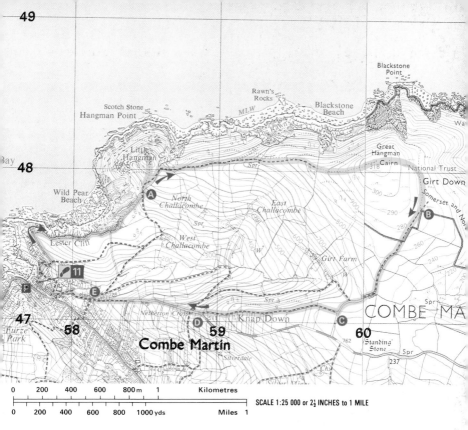

the Bristol Channel to South Wales. The large fifteenth-century church with an impressive 99 ft (30 m) tower is situated about a mile (1.5 km) inland from the harbour. Between the two stands Combe Martin's second most notable building – the Pack o' Cards Inn, built whimsically in the shape of a 'house' of cards.

The walk starts at Kiln car park above the harbour and the first 2 miles (3.25km) are uphill. Follow the direction of a coast path sign to take a tarmac track which climbs and bears right between houses, after which it degenerates into a rough track. Continue climbing up a series of steps between hedges and go through a metal gate – ahead is a daunting view of Little Hangman and, to the right, a rather less awesome view of Combe Martin strung out along its long, narrow valley. Keep ahead above Wild Pear Beach, dropping slightly to go through a gate and continuing down to another gate. Go through that and climb steeply up to Little Hangman, following coastal path signs. At the second footpath sign (A), you can make a short detour ahead for approximately 200 yards (184 m) to the summit of Little Hangman, from where there are spectacular views; otherwise turn right to continue along the coastal path, climbing somewhat more gently between bracken and gorse, over stiles and through gates, finally heading

across heathery moorland to the cairn that marks the summit of Great Hangman. The views from here, along the coast in both directions and inland over Exmoor, are magnificent.

Past the cairn the path starts to descend and bears right down to a wall corner and footpath sign (B). Here turn right, in the direction of the 'Path to County Road' sign, and head in a straight line over Girt Down, keeping roughly parallel with a wall on the left, to a stile. Climb over and continue, still by a wall on the left, through a gate; keep ahead through sheep pens and then along a broad, walled track that curves right downhill to a gate. Go through and continue along the track, soon turning right (C), at a footpath sign to 'Combe Martin via Knap Down Lane', along a narrow, hedge-lined path from which there are more superb views over Combe Martin Bay and Little Hangman.

After just over ½ mile (0.75 km) the path descends to a lane (D). Turn right along it for just over ¼ mile (0.5 km) to where it turns sharply to the left. Here keep ahead along a tree-lined track which descends to a road (E). Cross over and continue by the side of a house on the right, following a footpath sign 'Beach via Hangman Path', under a canopy of trees and over a brook. Turn left on joining a wider path and follow it down to a road where you turn right back to the harbour.

12 Brendon Forest

Start:	Luxborough (Pooltown)
Distance:	5½ miles (8.75 km)
Approximate Time:	3 hours
Parking:	Roadside verges near Luxborough or open space by road junction at Pooltown
Refreshments:	Pub at Luxborough
Ordnance Survey maps:	Landranger 181 (Minehead & Brendon Hills area) and Pathfinder SS 83/93 1235 (Exford & Brendon Hills (West))

General description *All the main characteristics of the Brendon Hills − a pleasantly varied mixture of conifer forests, deciduous woodlands, farmland, moorland and steep-sided combes − are included on this route. Although these rounded hills reveal a much gentler landscape than the wildness and openness of Exmoor proper, there is some reasonably steep and lengthy climbing on the walk, which explores part of the Brendon Forest area, ascending through plantations onto the open moorland of Withycombe Common, from where there are outstanding views over the coast and Quantock Hills. The descent offers equally spectacular views of the main Brendon ridge.*

The small and scattered village of Luxborough comprises three distinct sections: Church Town, by the church, and ½ mile (0.75 km) to the east the adjacent Kingsbridge, by the pub, and Pooltown. The walk begins at the road junction at Pooltown where you first head across the small area of open ground to the north and then continue along a narrow, wooded path by the little Washford River on the right. Turn left to keep by a tributary stream along the edge of Church Wood, bear right at a fork along the lower path through dense conifer woods, and on emerging from these there is a good view to the right of the isolated Luxborough church high up amidst fields and woods. Bear right on joining a lane **(A)** and follow it as it heads downhill, curves right and then heads up towards the church, a pleasant, mostly nineteenth-century building with a saddleback tower.

Take the first turning on the right and shortly afterwards turn left **(B)** up a tarmac drive between houses. Continue along a curving, uphill, hedge-lined track to go through a metal gate and then head downhill, passing a barn on the right. From this track there is a superb view to the right looking down a steep wooded combe to the main

Brendon Hills − a gentler landscape than the rest of Exmoor

ridge of the Brendon Hills beyond – a beautiful landscape of hills and woods, fields and hedges, greens and golds. Go through a gate, continue to a junction of tracks and turn left (C) uphill through conifers mixed with some hardwoods – part of Brendon Forest – to a complex junction of tracks and footpath sign at the top (D). Here keep straight ahead along the one track not indicated on the footpath sign across the heather, bracken and gorse of Withycombe Common, passing to the left of a triangulation pillar. From here the views are magnificent: Minehead, North Hill and across the Bristol Channel to the coast of South Wales to the left; Watchet, the Quantock ridge and the flatter coastal lands looking towards Weston-super-Mare to the right; and inland, looming over the tops of the dark array of conifers, the distinctive landmark of Dunkery Beacon.

Continue past the triangulation pillar along a broad track which heads down to a T-junction (E), turn right, between conifer woods on the right and the heathland of Rodhuish Common on the left, along another track up to a gate. Go through, continue across the field in front – there is no visible path – to go through a metal gate at the far end and keep along the edge of the next field by a hedge-bank on the left, bearing left and heading downhill. Go through another metal gate and bear right through a group of trees down to yet another gate.

Go through that, turn right along a lane to enter Druid's Combe Wood and after about 200 yards (184 m) bear left (F) along an almost parallel track which heads downhill keeping more or less in a straight line. Bear right on joining a drive and turn left over the Washford River to a lane (G). Turn right along the lane for ½ mile (0.75 km), keeping by the river and curving gradually left into Luxborough (Kingsbridge). Continue through the village for another ¼ mile (0.5 km) to the road junction at Pooltown.

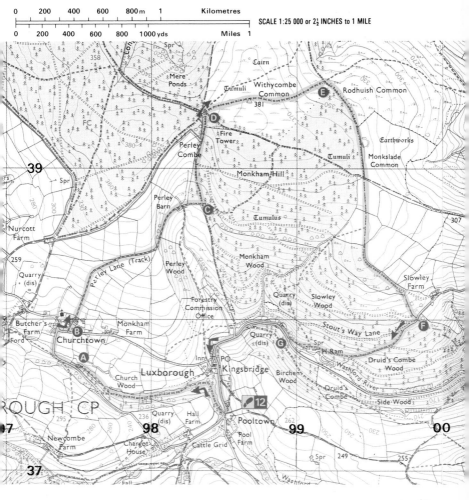

SCALE 1:25 000 or 2½ INCHES to 1 MILE

13 Exford and Room Hill

Start:	Exford
Distance:	6 miles (9.5 km)
Approximate Time:	3 hours
Parking:	Exford
Refreshments:	Pubs and cafés at Exford
Ordnance Survey maps:	Landranger 181 (Minehead & Brendon Hills area) and Pathfinder SS 83/93 1235 (Exford & Brendon Hills (West))

General description This walk goes through a most attractive stretch of the Exe valley to the south of the village of Exford. The first half of the route climbs over Road Hill and Room Hill, high above the valley, before descending to cross the river at Nethercote; the return keeps by the banks of

the Exe – a delightful riverside ramble that makes a fitting finale to a fine, scenic walk.

Exford, a spacious village with an attractive green, is almost in the geographical centre of Exmoor, surrounded by moorland. Its medieval church, heavily restored in the nineteenth century, stands high up on the eastern edge of the village, its tower visible from many points on the walk. Begin in the village car park where you pass through the kissing-gate at the far end to follow a red-waymarked route along the right-hand edge of a field, beside the river Exe on the right. Go through a gate and continue along this attractive riverside path, passing through another gate.

Turn right **(A)**, following footpath signs to Winsford Hill and Withypool, to cross the river and turn left at a 'Withypool via Room Hill' footpath sign to go along a winding tarmac lane which soon becomes a rough track. Where the lane bends sharply to the right keep ahead through a metal gate and along a stony track between hedge-banks,

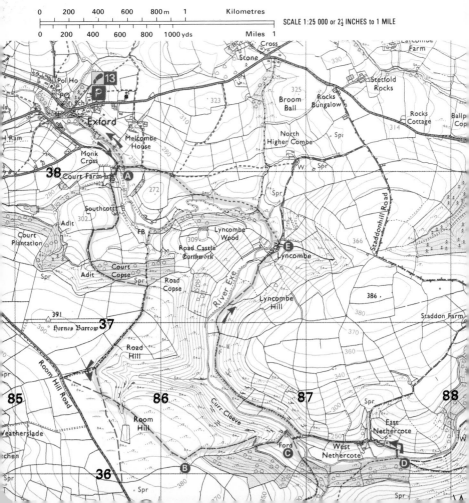

SCALE 1:25 000 or 2½ INCHES to 1 MILE

Exford from Room Hill

ascending steadily and later keeping by the edge of a field, with a wall and hedge on the left. Follow the field edge as it curves right, go through a metal gate and turn left, between a hedge on the left and a wire fence on the right, heading gently downhill into woodland. Go through a gate and continue, climbing quite steeply along the edge of Court Copse, to go through another gate. Continue across a field and to the left there is a superb view over Exford and the patchwork scene of fields, hedges and woodland on the slopes of the Exe valley. Go through another gate and turn right at a bridle-path sign, heading uphill over Road Hill along the edge of fields, by a hedge on the right; the view to the left, across bracken-covered slopes dotted with random trees is dominated by Winsford Hill. At a fork follow the left-hand path across the top of a combe on the left, continuing to a footpath sign. Bear left in the direction signposted Winsford across the open expanses of Room Hill — the path is not always visible on the ground but keep in a straight line — making towards a hedge on the right.

Just before reaching a metal gate beside the hedge bear left (**B**) and head downhill over rough grass and bracken, keeping parallel to a hedge on the right and soon joining a good, clear path which descends steeply into the Exe valley. At the bottom of the hill turn right beside the river (**C**), pass through a metal gate on the right and

continue along a yellow-waymarked concessionary path, by the pleasant tree-lined river-bank, passing through two gates and turning left over the river at Nethercote (**D**). Keep ahead along a farm track which curves left past East Nethercote Farm to a gate, go through and continue along the track past West Nethercote Farm. Now follows an easy and delightful 1½ mile (2.5 km) riverside walk to Lyncombe Farm along a most attractive, curving track, passing through a succession of gates. At first the track is wooded and enclosed by hedge-banks; later it continues through more open country, with glorious views across the Exe to the steep bracken-covered slopes on the other side.

At Lyncombe Farm go through a gate at the far end of the farm buildings and after a few yards turn left (**E**) through a yellow-waymarked gate. Turn right, at first along the right-hand edge of a field but later following yellow waymarks round to the left, to rejoin the river. Continue by the Exe over two stiles, through a metal gate and across the next field, keeping above the riverside meadows on the left. Pass through another gate and continue, climbing gently and later gradually bearing right across the middle of a field to a gate and stile in the far corner. Go through or climb over and bear left along a path, by a hedge on the right, to a stile and footpath sign (**A**). Climb over, turn right through a gate and retrace your steps following the river on the left into Exford.

14 Lynmouth and Watersmeet

Start:	Lynmouth
Distance:	6 miles (9.5 km)
Approximate Time:	3½ hours
Parking:	Lynmouth
Refreshments:	Pubs and cafés at Lynmouth, café at Watersmeet
Ordnance Survey maps:	Landranger 180 (Barnstaple & Ilfracombe) and Pathfinder SS 64/74 1214 (Lynton & Lynmouth)

General description *Here is one of the great classic walks of Exmoor: through the beautiful, steep-sided, thickly-wooded valleys of the East Lyn River and Hoaroak Water, most of which is now fortunately cared for by the National Trust. From the coastal village of Lynmouth the route follows the East Lyn as far as Watersmeet, then continues by Hoaroak Water, climbing up to Hillsford Bridge. The return route keeps along the top edge of the valleys, passing through more open country with spectacular views towards the coast. There are a number of steep 'ups and downs' on this section before the final descent into Lynmouth. Although the walk is of modest length there is quite a lot of climbing involved throughout, but take your time and enjoy it — the* sparkling rivers, magnificent woodlands and superb views repay the effort many times over.

After centuries as a remote and relatively unknown North Devon fishing village, Lynmouth was 'discovered' in the early nineteenth century. Its picturesque appearance and exceptionally attractive situation at the mouth of the little East Lyn and West Lyn rivers, sheltered by high cliffs on both sides, made it a favourite resort for aristocratic and intellectual visitors, followed by middle-class Victorian holidaymakers. In the twentieth century its popularity has further increased; it is easily reached from the nearby resorts of Ilfracombe and Minehead despite the hazards of Porlock and Countisbury Hills. The most dramatic and tragic event in Lynmouth's history was the flood disaster of August 1952, when, following exceptionally heavy rain on Exmoor, the swollen waters of the East Lyn and West Lyn surged through their narrow valleys, uprooting trees, destroying buildings and transporting boulders, to inflict severe damage on Lynmouth with the loss of over thirty lives.

The walk begins at Lyndale Cross car park, near the bridge over the East Lyn River. Take the path that runs beside the car park along the right bank of the river, keeping ahead at the first footbridge but turning left over the second one **(A)** to enter the National Trust property of Watersmeet. Turn right to follow the other bank through the enchanting, narrow, steep-sided, thickly-wooded East Lyn valley. Walking through this virtual

The lovely wooded valley of the East Lyn near Watersmeet

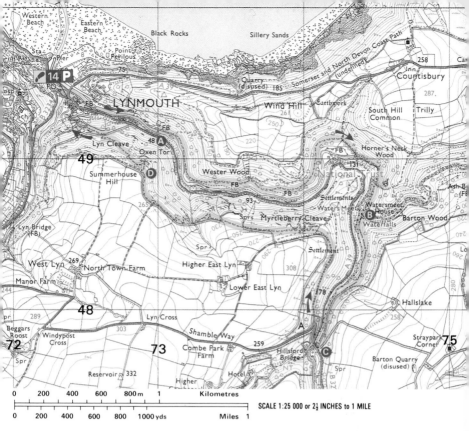

gorge, it is not difficult to envisage how much damage these rocky waters could do when greatly swollen with floodwater. At a fork bear slightly left along an uphill path, signposted 'Arnold's Linhay and Countisbury', and at the next footpath sign continue along the path signposted to Watersmeet and Rockford. Bear slightly left at the next fork, following directions to Watersmeet. From high up above the river the path curves right and descends to rejoin the river-bank, continuing to Watersmeet (B).

This is a charming spot and the waters that meet here are the East Lyn and Hoaroak Water. Cross the footbridge in front of Watersmeet House, originally built in the nineteenth century as a shooting and fishing lodge by the Halliday family, and now a National Trust shop and information centre with a convenient café. Turn right for a few yards and just before the next footbridge turn left along a path signposted 'Hillsford Bridge and Waterfall Viewpoint', climbing by a series of steps along the side of the valley of Hoaroak Water which is just as spectacularly attractive as that of the East Lyn River. At the top bear right to keep above the stream, soon passing the dramatic waterfall viewpoint on the right, and continue for ½ mile (0.75 km) to Hillsford Bridge (C). Turn right over the bridge, a relatively modern structure – the

earlier one was a casualty of the 1952 flood – and keep ahead at the road junction, along the road signposted to Blackmoor Gate, Barnstaple and Lynton.

Where there is a hairpin bend to the left, continue ahead at a National Trust sign along a path signposted to Lynmouth. Go through a gate and continue, climbing steadily through woodland and passing Myrtleberry South Iron Age settlement on the left, to emerge into open country, with the most superb views to the right across the East Lyn valley to the moorlands, and later to the coast beyond. Following footpath signs to Lynton and Lynmouth all the time, keep along the path which curves gradually to the left along the top edge of the valley and soon there are magnificent views ahead of Lynton and Lynmouth, and to the right of the prominent headland of The Foreland.

Pass through two gates in quick succession above Myrtleberry Cleave and from now on the route follows a whole series of sharp zigzag bends: first descending steeply to cross a stream, then ascending quite steeply, turning right at a footpath sign in the direction of Lynmouth (D), passing the rocks of Oxen Tor and descending steeply again, twisting and turning through the woods of Lyn Cleave. Finally the path continues between high stone walls, curving between cottages to descend into Lynmouth.

Selworthy – picturesque thatched cottages over-looking Dunkery Beacon

SAT

✓

15 Hurlstone and Selworthy Beacon

Start:	Bossington
Distance:	6½ miles (10.5 km)
Approximate Time:	3 hours
Parking:	Bossington
Refreshments:	Tea rooms at Bossington and Selworthy, café at Allerford
Ordnance Survey maps:	Landranger 181 (Minehead & Brendon Hills area) and Pathfinder SS 84/94 1215 (Minehead)

General description *Much of this walk is on land that was part of the Holnicote estate, formerly owned by the Acland family and given to the National Trust by Sir Richard Acland in 1944. The walk passes through three picturesque villages, and the countryside between them is some of the finest in Exmoor, combining a steep combe, open moorland and glorious woodland, with excellent views over the coast, the Vale of Porlock and inland to high Exmoor – the latter views dominated by Dunkery Beacon. The only climbing is at the start: a lengthy, steady and in places steep ascent along the side of Bossington Hill and up through Hurlstone Combe onto Selworthy Beacon – the finest of many fine viewpoints on a splendid and outstandingly attractive walk.*

Bossington is idyllic: a collection of thatched cottages sheltering at the foot of the steep, wooded slopes of Bossington Hill on the northern edge of the Vale of Porlock, ½ mile (0.75 km) from a beach and with a clear, sparkling stream running through it on its way to the sea. It is also an excellent walking centre.

Take the path that leads directly from the car park, at the footpath sign to Hurlstone and Selworthy, and cross a footbridge to a T-junction of paths. Turn left at a footpath sign to Hurlstone, by the stream on the left, following a path which curves right along the edge of woodland. After passing through a gate, the path starts to gradually climb between gorse and bracken to a stone indicating that this is the National Trust property of Hurlstone **(A)**. From here there is a lovely view to the left across Porlock Bay to Porlock and Porlock Weir; ahead is the commanding headland of Hurlstone Point.

Turn right, following coastal path signs to Minehead, now climbing much more steeply through Hurlstone Combe, a cleft between Hurlstone Point on the left and Bossington Hill on the right. The long, steep haul to the head of the combe rewards you with magnificent views to the right across the Vale or Porlock to the thickly-wooded valleys and moors beyond. At this point the coast path turns left but you keep straight ahead along a track to climb Selworthy Beacon (1012 ft (308 m)), from where the views – especially across the sea to the coast of South Wales and inland to Dunkery Beacon – are even more magnificent. Continue past the summit cairn and the National Trust stone down to a road **(B)**. Keep ahead along the road for a few yards and then bear right, at a footpath sign to Selworthy and Dunster, along a track, bearing right on meeting another track and heading gradually downhill. At the next footpath sign to Selworthy turn sharp right to continue more steeply downhill, curving through the beautiful woodland of Selworthy Combe, by a brook on the right, finally passing through a gate and onto a lane **(C)**.

To the left is Selworthy church, an imposing fourteenth- to fifteenth-century building, easily seen for miles around because of its distinctive white colour. It is periodically coated with a lime mixture to protect the stone from the weather – a practice that used to be more common in the past. The inside is particularly impressive for a small village church, with a fine, aisled nave and eighteenth-century gallery at its west end. From the south porch the view over the village to Dunkery is one of the finest in the area. Selworthy, which mainly comprises a number of thatched cottages grouped around a green, is remarkably picturesque and uniform – almost unreal in its perfection. It was purpose built by the Aclands of nearby Holnicote in the early nineteenth century for their retired tenants and estate workers.

Turn right by the cross in front of the church and walk across the charming and delightful Selworthy Green between the thatched cottages, rejoining the lane lower down to continue through the village. At the bottom end turn right along another lane, at a footpath sign to Allerford, passing a farm and continuing along a hedge-lined path to a fork. Here take the left-hand path, skirting woods on the right, down to a lane; continue along the narrow lane which curves left to drop down to the ford, cottage and old pack-horse bridge at Allerford **(D)**. This must be one of the most photographed scenes in the country, adorning literally thousands of calendars, birthday cards and chocolate boxes — undeniably idyllic and nostalgic, the town dweller's idealised view of rural life.

Cross the pack-horse bridge and turn right along the road through the village, turning right again at the far end along the drive to Stokes Farm **(E)**. Continue over a footbridge and at a footpath sign to West Lynch and Bossington turn left along a shady path, at first keeping by the stream on the left. The path later bears right uphill along the edge of the delightful woodland of Allerford Plantation, bearing left on meeting another path at a footpath sign to Bossington.

Immediately ahead is a fork: keep along the lower path, climb a stile and continue, passing through a gate at a path junction. Over to the left is Lynch chapel — you can make a slight detour to visit it by turning left at the footpath sign to West Lynch and Horner, just before the gate, and continue down to the road opposite the chapel. This fine, unaltered sixteenth-century building belonged to Athelney Abbey up to the closure of the monasteries in the 1530s and is believed to have been the chapel of the manor of Bossington.

After passing through the gate continue across a field, go through a gap in a wire fence and turn left along the right-hand edge of the next field down to a gate. Go through, continue down the steps ahead and turn right along a path through woodland which descends to another gate. Go through that and bear left to cross the footbridge back into Bossington.

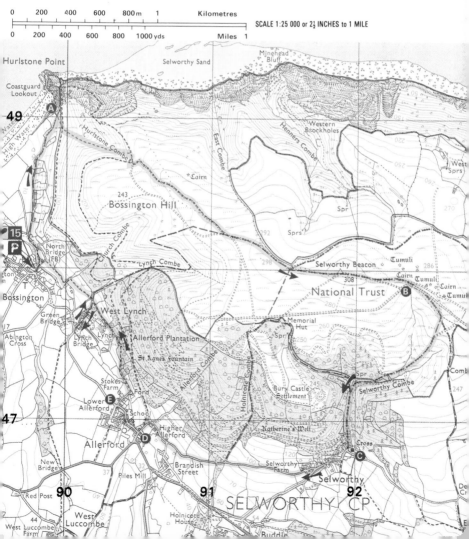

16 Hawkridge and Anstey Common

Start:	Hawkridge
Distance:	6 miles (9.5 km)
Approximate Time:	3½ hours
Parking:	Parking area at Hawkridge
Refreshments:	None
Ordnance Survey maps:	Landranger 181 (Minehead & Brendon Hills area), Pathfinders SS 83/93 1235 (Exford & Brendon Hills (West)) and SS 82/92 1256 (Dulverton)

General description *Two of the major components of the Exmoor landscape — wooded valleys and bare moorland — are combined in this walk on the southern edge of the National Park. Starting in the isolated, hilltop village of Hawkridge, the route proceeds along the ridge from which the village gets its name, high up above the valleys of the River Barle and Dane's Brook,* descending through the most delightful woodland to a point where river and brook meet. It continues through more woodland before climbing up to and heading across the open and exposed moorland of Anstey Common, then descending once more into the valley of Dane's Brook and finally climbing back up to the village. From the higher points the views are superb — recompense for the fair amount of climbing that is involved.

As its name suggests, the tiny, windswept village of Hawkridge stands nearly 1,000 ft (305 m) up on a ridge and is one of the highest and most isolated communities on Exmoor. The plain, simple church, which harmonises perfectly with its bleak surroundings — it has no windows on its exposed north side — dates mainly from the fourteenth and fifteenth centuries, although it retains a Norman south doorway.

From the village centre walk along the narrow lane signposted to Tarr Steps, passing the church on the right; where the lane bends sharply to the left keep ahead, at a footpath sign to Dulverton and East Anstey Common, along a hedge-lined track. Pass through two gates in quick succession and

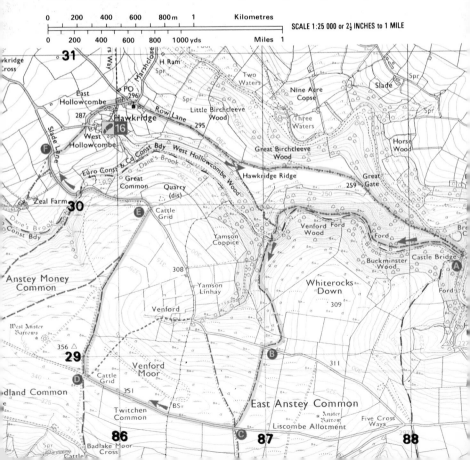

SCALE 1:25 000 or 2½ INCHES to 1 MILE

Hawkridge occupies an exposed position on the southern fringes of the moor

continue along the edge of a field, by a hedge-bank on the left, to a footpath sign in front of a gate. Go through the gate, following directions to Dulverton, to continue along Hawkridge ridge, from where there are fine views on both sides over the wooded valleys of the River Barle on the left and Dane's Brook on the right keeping between a wire fence on the left and a hedge-bank on the right. Pass through a gate and continue above Great Birchcleeve Wood, which slopes steeply down the side of the Barle valley, to go through another gate. Continue along a broad grassy path straight across the field ahead, descending to go through a gate at the edge of the woods. Now follow a path through this most attractive woodland, descending gently to a footpath sign and continuing downhill to a bridge, T-junction of paths and another footpath sign **(A)**. A few yards ahead Dane's Brook joins the Barle.

Turn sharp right along the banks of the brook, still through woodland and following yellow waymarks and footpath signs to Anstey Common all the while. After 1 mile (1.5 km) cross the brook to begin a steady climb through trees, emerging into more open country of gorse and bracken. Go through a gate, continue across an area of rough grass and bear right to pass through another gate and onto a road **(B)**. Cross over, go through a gate opposite at a footpath sign to East Anstey and continue along a broad grassy uphill path across the heather, scrub, gorse and bracken of East Anstey Common, passing through a metal gate onto another road **(C)**.

Turn right along this road for ¾ mile (1.25 km); there is a superb view to the left across the gentler farmlands of mid-Devon. At the end of the hedge-bank and trees on the right, just past a cattle grid, turn right **(D)** onto another area of open common, Anstey Money, following a broad track by a hedge-bank on the right. The track is marked by a Two Moors Way sign and a footpath sign to Hawkridge and descends to a road **(E)**, with fine views to the left of West Anstey Common and in front of Hawkridge.

Turn left, cross Dane's Brook and continue along the road which climbs steeply and curves right. Where it bends to the left **(F)** keep ahead through a gate at a Two Moors Way and Hawkridge footpath sign and walk across a field, veering left to go through a metal gate in the far left-hand corner. Turn right along a narrow, winding lane for the short distance into Hawkridge.

45

17 The Foreland and Countisbury Common

Start:	Countisbury
Distance:	7 miles (11.25 km)
Approximate Time:	3½ hours
Parking:	National Trust car park at Countisbury
Refreshments:	Pub at Countisbury
Ordnance Survey maps:	Landranger 180 (Barnstaple & Ilfracombe) and Pathfinder SS 64/74 1214 (Lynton & Lynmouth)

General description *Some of the finest coastal scenery in North Devon can be enjoyed on this walk, much of which is on National Trust property. Starting from the clifftop hamlet of Countisbury, the route heads over the fine viewpoint of Butter Hill to the prominent headland of The Foreland and then turns east to follow a particularly spectacular stretch of coast between Lynmouth and Porlock Bays along cliffs high above the sea, passing through delightful coastal woodlands. At the quaintly-named Desolation Point it turns inland and returns over the breezy, open, smooth slopes of Countisbury Common, from where the views over Exmoor emulate those along the coast.*

Countisbury comprises little more than a few cottages, an inn and a church situated at the top of the steep hill which plunges down into Lynmouth. The small, plain, sturdy church, high above the sea, looks as if it could withstand anything that the weather could throw at it. Just below it is the inn which was one of the stopping points on the horse-drawn coach journey between Minehead and Lynmouth; it took three hours and only ceased in 1913.

A gate leads from the car park onto a narrow lane; turn left along it, through the churchyard, passing to the left of the church and up to a stile **(A)**. Climb over, bear slightly right to a wall corner and continue along a grassy path, climbing gently to the top of Butter Hill (933 ft (302 m)), which is crowned by a television relay station. The all-round views from the triangulation pillar are magnificent: Lynmouth and Lynton, the coast of South Wales, Lundy Island, Porlock Bay and Hurlstone Point, and inland over the wooded hills, valleys and open moorlands of Exmoor.

Continue straight ahead, descending gently to a wall and a T-junction of paths.

Turn left, keeping by a wall and wire fence on the right, head steeply downhill to a footpath sign and continue in the direction signposted 'Coast Path and Lighthouse' towards The Foreland. At the next 'Coast Path and Lighthouse' footpath sign turn right to continue along the side of Butter Hill, with The Foreland on the left, descending steeply into the narrow, bare, scree-covered slopes of Coddow Combe, turning sharp left down to the narrow, tarmac road which links the lighthouse on The Foreland with the A39 **(B)**. The view ahead is dominated by the razor-sharp looking rocks of Warmersturt. Turn right along the road, following a 'Coast Path and County Road' footpath sign, cross a footbridge and continue uphill through the combe.

Where the road bends sharply to the right keep ahead at a coast path sign, along a track, curving right to a gate and stile. Climb over, turn right up some steps and turn left at the next coast path sign. Now follows a superlative coastal walk of 1½ miles (2.5 km) much of which is through the steep-sided and delightful Chubhill Wood, passing through several gates on the way. Turn inland slightly to cross wooded Dogsworthy Combe and continue to the next combe, near Desolation Point **(C)**.

Here cross a stream and immediately turn

right, at a footpath sign to Whitegate and County Gate, along a steep, winding, narrow and rather overgrown path — fortunately there are regular yellow waymarks — through the wooded Wingate Combe, later keeping by a wire fence on the right and passing through a gate. Continue uphill to the top of the combe and keep ahead, by a hedge-bank and wire fence on the right, still climbing and continuing up to a stile. Climb over, keep ahead through a plantation, pass through a gate at the far end and bear right at a footpath sign 'Black Gate and County Gate'. To the left are the earthworks of the Roman fortlet of Old Barrow, a first century AD signal station, probably built to guard this part of the coast from raids by the Silures tribe from South Wales. Walk along the track that bears right across open grassland, keeping parallel to a hedge-bank and wire fence on the right and later continuing between hedge-banks and a series of gates to the A39 (**D**).

Turn right along the main road for ½ mile (0.75 km) — there is a fine view of Countisbury Common ahead — and at a footpath sign to Countisbury (**E**) turn right over a stile to follow a yellow-waymarked route along the right-hand edge of two fields to join a broad track. Where the track turns right through a gate, bear slightly left, in the direction of a Countisbury footpath sign, away from the hedge-bank on the right, pass through a gate in the wire fence ahead and

The glorious view over Lynton and Lynmouth from The Foreland

continue over Countisbury Common. Pass through three more gates, keeping parallel with the hedge-bank on the right, and continue, by a wire fence on the right, across a field above Kipscombe Farm, bearing right through a metal gate. Cross the farm drive and at a Countisbury footpath sign keep ahead to join a grassy track. Go through a gate, cross the 'lighthouse road' (**F**) and continue over heather and gorse, bearing slightly left at a fork. To the left is the prehistoric burial site of Barna Barrow. After joining a hedge-bank on the left, keep along it to head downhill — with superb views of Countisbury church and beyond that Lynton and Lynmouth — finally bearing left to the stile in the church wall. Retrace your steps through the churchyard to the car park.

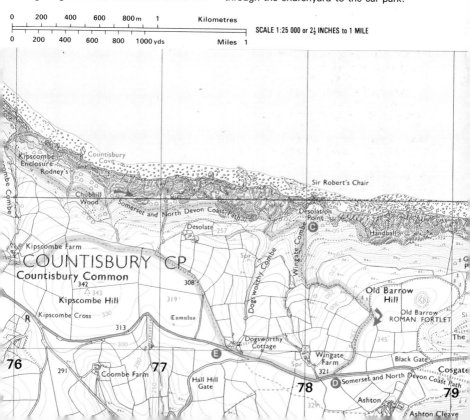

18 Winsford Hill

Start:	Winsford
Distance:	7 miles (11.25 km)
Approximate Time:	3½ hours
Parking:	Winsford
Refreshments:	Pub and cafés at Winsford
Ordnance Survey maps:	Landranger 181 (Minehead & Brendon Hills area) and Pathfinder SS 83/93 1235 (Exford & Brendon Hills (West))

General description To the south-west of Winsford rises Winsford Hill, at 1399 ft (426 m) not the highest but certainly one of the most prominent of Exmoor hills: an open and breezy expanse of gorse and heather above the valley of the River Exe and a magnificent viewpoint. The walk climbs through woodland from the village to the summit of the hill, then descends along the rim of the spectacular valley called The Punchbowl, climbing again over Bye Hill for a final ramble along the top edge of the steep-sided Exe valley before descending through more woodland back to Winsford.

Winsford has been described as the prettiest village in Exmoor, one of a large number that compete for that accolade. With its combination of attractive cottages, thatched inn, ford and seven bridges – including an old pack-horse bridge – it certainly has an outstanding claim. On a slight eminence to the west of the village stands the medieval church, its fine, tall tower dominating both village and surrounding area. Perhaps unusually – as such idyllic surroundings are not normally associated with the turbulent world of either industrial or international relations – Winsford was the birthplace in 1881 of Ernest Bevin, founder of the Transport and General Workers' Union, leading World War II statesman and Foreign Secretary in the 1945-51 Labour Government.

In the centre of Winsford take the road

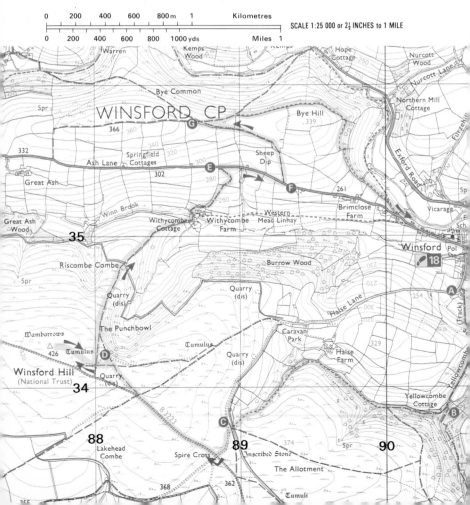

SCALE 1:25 000 or 2½ INCHES to 1 MILE

Looking over The Punchbowl from Winsford Hill

signposted to Tarr Steps, passing the war memorial and thatched Royal Oak Inn, heading uphill. At a footpath sign to Dulverton, Tarr Steps and Winsford Hill **(A)** turn left along a track which soon bears right and ascends, enclosed by trees and hedges; gaps in the hedges reveal lovely views to the left over Winsford and the Exe valley. The track enters attractive woodland and then descends gently to a gate just before a brook. Go through the gate and, ignoring the stile on the left, keep ahead **(B)**, passing Yellowcombe Cottage on the right, along a narrow but discernible path which curves right and heads steadily uphill through a narrow, wooded valley, keeping by the brook on the right for most of the way. After 1 mile (1.5 km) you emerge from the trees and continue ahead across bracken and grass to go through a metal gate and onto a road a few yards ahead near the top of Winsford Hill **(C)**. A short distance to the east of here, along the path which comes in from the left just before reaching the road, is the Caractacus Stone, covered by a stone shelter. It is inscribed 'Carataci Nepus' (kinsman of Caractacus) and is the only example of an inscribed standing stone in the area. Its age is a mystery; it was possibly erected by a local chieftain during that twilight period of the Dark Ages when Roman power in Britain was on the wane.

Turn left to a junction (Spire Cross) where you turn right along a road signposted to Simonsbath and Lynton, Exford and Withypool, which climbs gently. Where the road bears slightly left to bisect the obvious tracks on both sides of it, bear right along a grassy path across heather and bracken that has superb views all around and is pleasantly fresh and open after the previous confines of the wooded valley. There are many paths and tracks across the National Trust property of

Winsford Hill, but at the next path junction bear left and, at the one after that, **(D)** continue ahead, climbing gently along a broad grassy path that heads straight to the summit; this is marked by a stone next to three Bronze Age burial chambers called the Wambarrows. From here the magnificent 360-degree views take in much of Exmoor and on a clear day even the edge of Dartmoor can be seen.

Retrace your steps to the first junction of paths **(D)** and here turn sharp left along a path which runs above the steep-sided, bracken-covered slopes of The Punchbowl on the right, from which there are spectacular views across the combe to rolling hills beyond. Follow a yellow-waymarked route along the edge of the combe, descending into the valley of Winn Brook and bearing right to go through a gate and along the edge of a field, by a line of trees and a hedge-bank on the right. Near the bottom of the field go through a gap by a yellow-topped post and continue, now with a line of trees and a hedge-bank on the left, down to a metal gate. Go through and keep along a track which makes a hairpin bend to the left, crosses Winn Brook and continues to Withycombe Farm. Pass through the farm buildings, turn right along a tarmac drive, go through a gate and follow the winding farm drive up to a road **(E)**.

Turn right for ¼ mile (0.5 km) (be careful – it is narrow and has no verges) and just before the road veers slightly to the left there are two gates on the left, side by side **(F)**. Go through the left-hand, wooden, one and head up the right-hand edge of a field, with a hedge on the right, to pass through a gate at the top. Turn left along the edge of the next two fields, by a hedge and wire fence on the left, climbing gently up Bye Hill and, in the second field, looking out for a footpath sign and red-waymarked stone a few yards to the right **(G)**. Here turn sharp right, following directions for Winsford, back across the field to go through a metal gate in the left-hand corner.

Continue along a delightful path above the steep-sided Exe valley, keeping ahead along the top path at a fork, to a gate. Go through and continue by a wire fence on the right, turning right through the next gate and immediately turning left through another gate along the top edge of woodland. Soon Winsford village and church are in sight. Follow the path to the left at a footpath sign, turn right through a gate and continue through the trees, descending steadily to another gate. Go through that and keep ahead (do not turn left at a red-waymarked footpath sign) to pass through a metal gate onto a lane. Bear left for the short distance back to Winsford.

19 Simonsbath and the River Barle

Start:	Simonsbath
Distance:	7 ½ miles (12 km)
Approximate Time:	4 hours
Parking:	Simonsbath
Refreshments:	Hotel at Simonsbath
Ordnance Survey maps:	Landrangers 180 (Barnstaple & Ilfracombe) and 181 (Minehead & Brendon Hills area), Pathfinders SS 63/73 (Bratton Fleming & Brayford) and SS 83/93 1235 (Exford & Brendon Hills (West))

General description *The whole length of the River Barle is delightful and no stretch more so than that downstream from Simonsbath – glorious woodland soon giving way to a peaceful, remote, steep-sided and bracken-covered valley. The first part of the walk follows the river-bank, passing such diverse man-made remains as a prehistoric earthwork and the ruins of a nineteenth-century copper mine; the second part returns high above the valley, giving superb views all the way.*

Simonsbath is situated in the heart of the old Royal Forest of Exmoor and until the early nineteenth century its only building was the residence of the Warden of the Forest, built in the seventeenth century and now a hotel. When the forest was sold off in 1818 it was purchased by John Knight, a Worcestershire industrialist, and it was he and his family who were responsible for constructing walls, building roads, planting trees and transforming many areas of moorland into farmland. Simonsbath's early nineteenth-century church, Birchcleave Wood and the Wheal Eliza Mine – passed near the start of the walk – are three examples of their varied activities, in the latter case an unsuccessful one.

The walk starts just above Simonsbath Bridge, opposite the Exmoor Forest Hotel, where you go through a gate at a footpath sign to Wheal Eliza, Cow Castle, Landacre and Withypool. Keep ahead uphill a few yards to another footpath sign where the path forks, and take the right-hand fork along a yellow-waymarked route signposted 'Landacre via Cow Castle' through the lower slopes of the delightful Birchcleave Wood above the river. Despite its name it is a beech wood, one of the highest in the country

(1300 ft (396 m)), mostly planted by the Knight family in the mid-nineteenth century. After emerging from the wood continue along a path by the Barle for the next 2 ½ miles (4 km) through a wild, lonely but lovely landscape, negotiating a series of gates and stiles and following yellow waymarks all the time. The views down the steep, bracken-covered slopes of the river valley are outstanding. You keep above or beside the Barle all the way except for two minor diversions. The first is where you bear left around the base of the prominent hill of Flexbarrow, rejoining the river by the scanty ruins of Wheal Eliza **(A)**, an unsuccessful copper mine developed by the Knights that was in operation only from 1846 to 1857. The second diversion, a longer one, is around the base of the prominent, conical-shaped hill topped by the earthworks of Cow Castle, an Iron Age fort.

After proceeding along the right-hand edge of a plantation the path starts to climb

steadily across bracken and heather, high above and bearing away from the river, heading up towards the top of the ridge. At this point there is a fine view to the right over wild and uninhabited country to Landacre Bridge. On reaching the ridge **(B)** turn sharp left, at a footpath sign 'Simonsbath via Picked Stones', to now follow a red-waymarked route along the top edge of the valley, with magnificent views all the way. Go through a gate, bear left along the edge of a field, with a hedge-bank on the left, to go through another gate and turn left down a tarmac farm track, through a metal gate and on towards the farm. Pass through another metal gate, continue in front of Pickedstones Farm and on through two more gates. Bear right, by a hedge-bank on the right, and continue through a series of gates, with at one stage a dramatic view of the earthworks of Cow Castle below, descending to cross a stream, White Water, and climbing up the other side of the valley. Nearing the top of a ridge bear left between gateposts and then bear right along the edge of a field, by a hedge-bank and small plantation on the right, continuing by the hedge-bank through three more gates. Just before a fourth gate bear left **(C)** and continue along the right-hand edge of a field, following the field edge round

The River Barle flows below the slopes of beautiful Birchcleave Wood

to the left, by a wire fence on the right, making for a gate.

Go through and continue, by a hedge-bank and wire fence on the right, through three more gates and then bear left, now with a hedge-bank on the left, to another gate. Pass through that and another one a few yards ahead, continuing downhill along the edge of a field, by a hedge-bank on the right, and through another gate to re-enter Birchcleave Wood. Bear left along a path through the wood, bearing right at a footpath sign and heading downhill back to Simonsbath. On this final stretch of the walk comes one more outstanding and memorable view: looking down through the trees on the left to the river and Simonsbath Bridge.

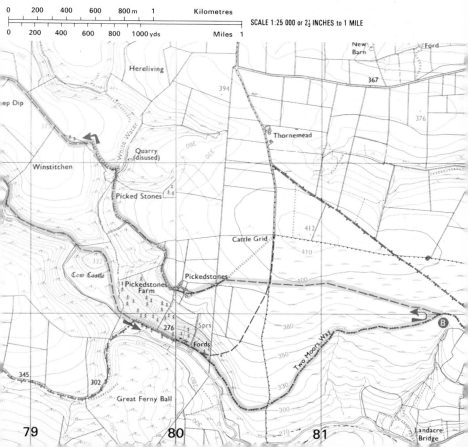

20 Haddon Hill and Wimbleball Lake

Start:	Haddon Hill
Distance:	6½ miles (10.5 km)
Approximate Time:	3½ hours
Parking:	Haddon Hill
Refreshments:	None
Ordnance Survey maps:	Landranger 181 (Minehead & Brendon Hills area) and Pathfinder SS 82/92 1256 (Dulverton)

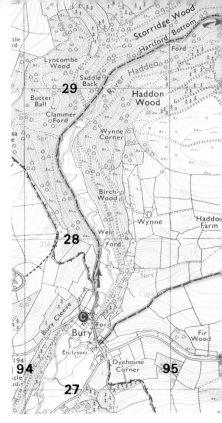

General description *The view across Wimbleball Lake at the start, and for the first ½ mile (0.75 km) or so of the walk to the summit of Haddon Hill, dispels the myth that reservoirs are inevitably unattractive intrusions in the landscape. Indeed here in Exmoor, which lacks any natural lakes, a large expanse of water such as this could be said to enhance it. From the top of Haddon Hill the route descends through woodland, via a superb enclosed lane, into the lovely Haddeo valley at Bury; then comes a magnificent woodland walk of nearly 3 miles (4.75 km), initially by the river and later above the reservoir, before returning to the starting point. Any climbing involved is gradual and there is very much an off-the-beaten-track feel to this walk which passes through two sleepy hamlets.*

As the car park is fairly high up there are immediate fine views looking across Wimbleball Lake to the village of Brompton Regis near the lake's left bank. There was opposition when the reservoir was built in the 1970s but skilful landscaping and the passage of time have given it a more natural appearance, especially when viewed from Haddon Hill.

Turn left at a footpath sign to Haddon Hill and make for a gate in the far corner of the car park. Go through the gate, keep ahead for about 50 yards (46 m) to a red and yellow marker post and bear left to follow a broad track across bracken, gorse and heather, climbing gently over Haddon Hill (1,160 ft (355 m)), with superb panoramic views. Continue past the triangulation pillar, which is a few yards to the left, for ¼ mile (0.5 km) and turn left **(A)** along an obvious path through the heather, making for the corner of Hadborough Plantation ahead and continuing along a broad downhill track by the right-hand edge of the plantation. Go through a gate, bear slightly left and continue downhill, between woodland on the right and the wire fence bordering the plantation on the left, to go through another gate. A few

yards ahead turn right **(B)** along a most attractive tree-lined track that heads downhill, emerges from the trees and continues to Haddon Farm.

*The first section of the walk from the car park to **(A)** follows an Exmoor National Park permissive path. This path may be closed from time to time in the interests of conservation and if so there is an alternative route which follows a public right of way, joining the walk at **(B)**. For this alternative, leave the car park by the entrance, turn right past a lodge, and then right again down a track. After about ¾ mile (1.25 km), just as the conifer hedge on the left of the track ends, turn left and go through a gate. Walk*

Wimbleball Lake from Haddon Hill

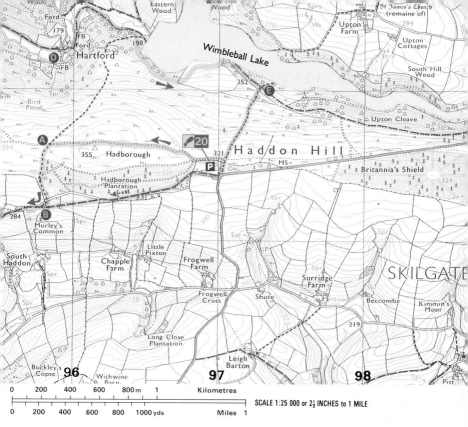

straight across a field to go through another gate here joining the main route and continuing to Haddon Farm.

Go through a gate, walk between the farm buildings and then turn half-left down to another gate. Go through that and continue along a downhill track enclosed by hedge-banks and trees — it is likely to be overgrown — which bears right and continues through a metal gate. From here there are fine views through gaps in the trees on the right of the steep-sided, thickly-wooded Haddeo valley. Go through another metal gate and continue down the enclosed track to pass through a gate and a few yards ahead turn right along a lane into the beautiful and quiet hamlet of Bury, proceeding to the fine old bridge by the ford over the River Haddeo **(C)**.

Cross the bridge, bear right along a narrow tarmac lane and go through a gate at a bridle-way sign to Hartford and Upton to continue along a wooded track called Lady Harriet Acland's Drive, which follows the valley of the winding river, and later the reservoir, for 4 miles (6.5 km) to Upton. This fairly level, well surfaced track, constructed to commemorate the devotion of Lady Harriet Acland, who nursed her husband to health after he was wounded as a prisoner of the French in the American War, keeps along the wooded banks of the river to the hamlet of Hartford

(D). Here keep ahead at a bridle-way sign to Upton Dam and Haddon Hill, go through the gate of Hartford Mill and turn left in front of a house. Before the next gate turn right along the left-hand side of a lawn to the river where you turn left along the bank for about 50 yards (46 m) and then turn right over a footbridge. Now turn left along the other bank of the river to a gate; go through and keep ahead, bearing slightly right to join a concrete water authority road and continuing to a gate by a cattle-grid. Go through and continue along the road, now with the river on your left, and at a fork keep ahead along the uphill road, climbing to the top of the right-hand side of the dam. Continue to another gate by a cattle-grid, go through and keep ahead, still walking uphill, to a footpath sign.

Here turn left along a track, signposted to Upton, which heads downhill to a gate. Go through to rejoin Lady Harriet's Drive, which curves left down towards the lake and then bears right alongside it, passing through a gate into woodland. The next part of the walk is particularly attractive as the pleasant grassy track continues through the wood, with the waters of the lake sparkling through the trees below on the left — at this point the lake becomes quite narrow. On reaching a tarmac track **(E)**, turn right at a footpath sign and follow the track uphill for just under ½ mile (0.75 km) back to the starting point.

21 Parracombe and Challacombe Commons

Start:	St Petrock's Church, on the A39 near Parracombe
Distance:	8½ miles (13.5 km)
Approximate Time:	4 hours
Parking:	Parking in the narrow lanes of Parracombe is impossible, therefore park on any convenient verges beside or just off the A39 near St Petrock's Church
Refreshments:	Pub at Parracombe
Ordnance Survey maps:	Landranger 180 (Barnstaple & Ilfracombe) and Pathfinder SS 64/74 1214 (Lynton & Lynmouth)

General description *This walk crosses the wide, high, open country roughly between the villages of Parracombe and Challacombe near the western fringes of Exmoor. Although it lies between the busy A39 and the almost equally busy B3358, this area has a very remote and lonely atmosphere. Parracombe Common is now mostly enclosed and given over to farmland; Challacombe Common remains in part as a remnant of the old, wild Exmoor. On such open country the views are inevitably extensive and impressive and most of the climbs, though lengthy, are both gradual and modest.*

Walk along the broad, hedge-lined track opposite the notice to St Petrock's Church; the track curves slightly right to a gate, just in front of which the track forks. Do not go through the gate but take the left-hand fork, turn right at a T-junction of tracks in front of a house and soon turn left to climb steadily to another T-junction (**A**). Here turn right along a straight tarmac drive and follow it for the next 1¼ miles (2 km) over Parracombe Common. After a while the drive becomes a rough track that curves gradually to the right, gently climbing the ridge to a gate at the top.

Go through the gate and keep straight ahead — there is no obvious path — across the open and sometimes boggy moorland of Challacombe Common, with splendid and extensive views all around, looking out for a metal gate in the wall ahead. Go through it and continue, beside a wall topped by a

hedge on the right, in a straight line through three gates, heading gradually downhill. After passing through the third gate keep along the left-hand side of a field by a hedge on the left, passing Withycombe Farm about 200 yards (184 m) to the right, to go through another metal gate. Keep ahead, passing through one more metal gate, and continue downhill along a concrete farm road to the B3358 (**B**).

Cross over the road, go through a gate opposite and a few yards to the left, and walk along the left-hand edge of a field, by a hedge on the left, bearing slightly right to go through a gate at the end of the field. Bear right, head uphill to the top right-hand corner of the next field and go through a gate on the left. Continue along the right-hand edge of a field, with a wall and hedge on the right, turning right through a gate at the end of the field and bearing slightly left along a hedge-lined path, heading directly towards the hamlet of Barton Town and the tower of Challacombe church. The church is in an isolated position, nearly a mile (1.5 km) to the west of the village of Challacombe. Although of medieval origin, it was mostly rebuilt around the middle of the nineteenth century.

Pass to the right of the church, go through two gates and keep ahead a few yards to go through a third gate onto a lane (**C**). Turn right along the lane for nearly ¾ mile (1.25 km), first descending and then climbing to recross the B3358 at Yelland Cross (**D**). Continue along a tarmac track signposted to Whitefield, following it as it bends right, at a yellow-waymarked bridle-way sign 'Highley and A39'. Turn left in front of Whitefield Barton Farm and continue, passing through a gate and curving first left and then right, to go through a metal gate at a bridle-way sign. Now keep along a track called Town Close Lane, parallel with a hedge-bank on the left, which climbs gently along the left-hand edge of a field, turns left through a gate and then turns right to continue uphill, along the right-hand edge of the next field. Turn right through a gate at the top and continue along the edge of the next field, once more with a hedge-bank on the left, climbing over the rough and open grassland of Challacombe Common again.

Pass through a metal gate, continue across the rough terrain to go through another gate and keep ahead to pass between redundant gateposts, bearing slightly left between hedge-banks down to a gate. Go through that and in front is probably the finest view of the walk — looking down the steep, partly-wooded, bracken-covered slopes of the combe watered by the Heddon River to a lovely patchwork of fields, hedges and trees, with Parracombe village ahead and on the horizon the headlands of the North Devon

The houses of Parracombe climb up the steep slopes of the valley of the little River Heddon

coast. Continue across bracken and gorse — there is not always a clear path — along the top right-hand edge of the combe, keeping roughly parallel with a wire fence on the right, and head downhill to go through a gate. Continue along the edge of the next field, with a hedge-bank on the left, pass through a gap at the end of it and keep ahead along the edge of the next one, turning left through a gate at the bottom end. Immediately turn right through another gate to follow a track beside the wooded combe on the left, descending to a gate. Go through and head steeply uphill, curving first right and then sharp left to reach the A39 **(E)**.

Cross over the road and go through a gate opposite, at a footpath sign to Parracombe, to follow a yellow-waymarked path across a field. Pass through two sets of gateposts, between which you cross the track of the disused Lynton-Barnstaple railway, and continue across the next field, making for the far right-hand corner. Here go through a gate and continue along an enclosed track for about 100 yards (92 m) before turning left through a gate at a yellow waymark. Bear right and follow the edge of a field over a brook a few yards ahead and then bear left, heading across to and joining a hedge-bank on the right, continuing to a footpath sign and gate. Go through and walk along a

hedge-lined track, passing through a metal gate in front of a farm. Immediately turn left through another metal gate, turn right at the side of a barn, go through a gate at the end of the barn and continue across the next field in the direction of Parracombe church to go through a gate in the far left-hand corner. Bear right over a brook and bear left to climb a stile in the hedge-bank ahead onto a lane.

The village of Parracombe, lying half-hidden in the steep valley of the River Heddon, is to the left; the route continues by turning right and following the lane to a T-junction **(F)**. Here turn right in the direction sign-posted 'Church Town and Old Church' along a narrow, uphill, winding, enclosed lane which curves right over a disused railway bridge. Afterwards it becomes a rough track which continues past the redundant St Petrock's Church on the left up to the main road and starting point.

The mainly fifteenth-century church was made redundant in 1879 when a new church was built on a new site in the centre of the village, as the old church was thought to be unstable. Proposals to demolish it caused widespread protests, led by John Ruskin, and St Petrock's was spared and subsequently restored — very fortunately as it is an imposing building with a rare and completely unspoilt Georgian interior.

22 Quantock combes and ridge

Start:	Holford
Distance:	8½ miles (13.5 km)
Approximate Time:	4½ hours
Parking:	Holford Green (Turn off the A39 down the lane between the Plough Inn and the garage, bear right at the signpost to Hodder's Combe and the car park is in the trees on the left)
Refreshments:	Pub and tea rooms at Holford
Ordnance Survey maps:	Landranger 181 (Minehead & Brendon Hills area) and Pathfinder ST 04/14 1216 (Watchet)

General description 'Upon smooth Quantock's airy ridge we roved Unchecked, or loitered 'mid her sylvan combes'. These lines by William Wordsworth illustrate the two most outstanding physical features of the Quantock Hills: the broad, smooth ridge and the steep-sided, thickly-wooded combes that fall away from it on both sides to some exquisite villages that lie at their feet. The walk starts at one of those villages and crosses three of the combes before climbing to the ridge at Crowcombe Park Gate. Then follows an invigorating 2¼ mile (3.5 km) walk along the 'airy ridge' to Bicknoller Post, before descending and returning to the starting point via the impressive Holford Beeches. This part of the Quantocks is very much Wordsworth's 'other country': he and his sister Dorothy lived for a year at nearby Alfoxton (1797-8) and they and fellow poet Coleridge, who lived nearby at Nether Stowey, frequently met to roam over these hills, which are a paradise for walkers.

Refer to map overleaf.

Holford, a pleasant little village lying at the foot of wooded combes below the eastern slopes of the Quantocks, has an attractive nineteenth-century church with a saddleback tower, thatched cottages and a quiet green edged with trees. It is from the car park at the side of the green that the walk begins.

Turn right along the road and bear left up to a junction, where you turn sharp right

Holford Beeches, below the Quantock ridge

along a lane signposted to Holford Combe. Follow this lane past houses and cottages, later passing Combe House Hotel on the right, after which the lane degenerates into a rough track (A). Continue along this track up through the lovely Holford Combe, steep-sided and thickly-wooded with pleasant grassy clearings at intervals. Cross and re-cross the stream several times but keep by it all the while to the point where it divides, just before a junction of three tracks (B). Here turn left to continue more steeply up through Lady's Combe, turning right at a T-junction of paths near the top to a lane a few yards ahead (C). Cross over and take the path ahead, climbing more gently now through trees, heather and bracken, with lovely views to the left across the coast and Somerset Levels to the line of the Mendips on the horizon. After ½ mile (0.75 km) you reach a road.

Turn left for about 300 yards (276 m) and at the first path on the right (D) turn sharply, almost doubling back, to follow a narrow but clear path through trees, bracken and heather, bearing left on joining a broad track and heading downhill through thick woodland. In a short while bear right off the track onto a narrower path and after 50 yards (46 m) bear right again to join another broad track. Continue downhill through trees, curving left into the conifer plantations of Rams Combe and later bearing right to join a broad forest track (E). Turn right along the track, climbing steadily between the tall and impressive Douglas firs of Rams Combe, by a stream on the left. Bear left on joining another track, go through a gate and continue across heather and bracken to the road and parking area at Crowcombe Park Gate (F).

Cross the road and keep ahead to a junction of tracks where you bear slightly right to join the Quantock ridge path. Now follows a superlative walk of 2¼ miles (3.5 km) along the crest of the Quantocks to Bicknoller Post, across a broad expanse of

bracken, gorse and heather. The views are magnificent: to the left across to the Brendon Hills and to the right over steep combes to Bridgwater Bay. Later there are equally impressive views: ahead across the channel to South Wales, and to the left Minehead can be seen, backed by North Hill and beyond that the rolling hills of Exmoor. Prehistoric burial sites punctuate the route. There are several broad tracks that run roughly parallel across the ridge, all eventually meeting at Bicknoller Post – which is actually identified by a post. This is a veritable 'Spaghetti Junction' of paths and tracks (G).

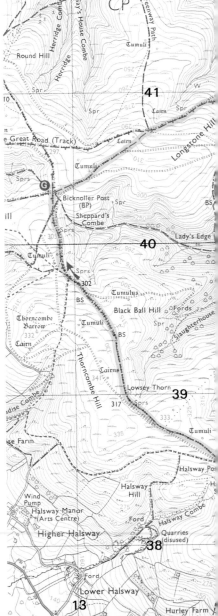

View from the Quantock ridge

Turn half-right along a narrow but obvious path, heading in a straight line in a north-easterly direction, passing a heather-covered tumulus on the left and joining a track on the right. Keep along this track, bearing left at a fork and heading downhill to a marker post. Now bear right along another broad track, following directions to Holford, towards the trees ahead **(H)**.

Continue along the right-hand edge of the trees, following directions for Holford on another marker post, heading downhill through the lovely Holford Beeches, lines of large, magnificent, ancient gnarled beeches — a most enjoyable finale to a splendid walk. Over to the left are the grounds of Alfoxton Park; it was Alfoxton House, now a hotel and much enlarged, that the Wordsworths rented during their year-long stay in the Quantocks. After nearly 1 mile (1.5 km) you reach a lane; continue along it as it curves right past Holford Green back to the car park.

SCALE 1:25 000 or 2½ INCHES to 1 MILE

23 Porlock, Horner Wood and Stoke Pero

Start:	Porlock
Distance:	7 ½ miles (12 km)
Approximate Time:	4 hours
Parking:	Porlock
Refreshments:	Pubs and cafés at Porlock
Ordnance Survey maps:	Landranger 181 (Minehead & Brendon Hills area) and Pathfinder SS 84/94 1215 (Minehead)

General description *Some beautiful stretches of woodland, narrow combes, sparkling streams, open moorland and tremendous views over coast, vale and moor – and a most attractive old village and an isolated church – all add up to an extremely varied and interesting walk. It is also a fairly energetic walk, involving several steep climbs, but it is undeniably worth the effort.*

At one time Porlock was on the coast but the sea has long receded and it is now nearly a mile (1.5 km) inland, situated in a fertile vale at the foot of steep, wooded hills. Its position – on a main road and close to hills, moors, woods and coast – makes it an excellent touring and walking centre and it has plenty of pubs, cafés and shops to cater for visitors. Immediately to the west the A39 climbs up the notorious Porlock Hill (1 in 4 and with hairpin bends), one of the steepest sections of main road in the country, its downward route peppered with warning signs and escape lanes. Porlock is a most attractive village, with some interesting buildings: notably the Old Ship Inn, fifteenth-century Doverhay Court (now a museum and tourist information centre) and the handsome thirteenth-century church, built of the local warm sandstone and dedicated to St Dubricius, an early Welsh bishop – evidence of the close cross-channel ties between Somerset and South Wales during the Dark Ages. Outside, its most distinguishing feature is the curiously truncated spire and inside it contains some outstanding tombs and monuments.

Start by the church, walking along the path at the side of it called The Drang to a junction of paths. Turn right through a kissing-gate and continue along a road for a few yards to a T-junction, where you turn right along a lane called Doverhay. Follow this lane for ¼ mile (0.5 km) – after leaving the houses of Porlock it becomes very narrow – keeping ahead at a junction signposted to West Luccombe and proceeding uphill. Just before a right-hand bend turn right (**A**), at a footpath sign to Ley Hill and Stoke Pero, onto a narrow path that heads up through thick woodland, turning right on joining a wider path. Continue along that path, which later narrows and at times becomes overgrown and quite difficult, eventually climbing steeply up through a dark and gloomy plantation. Turn left, now climbing much less steeply, to go through a gate and ahead to a lane.

Turn right along this narrow, uphill lane for about ¼ mile (0.5 km), bearing left (**B**), at a sign saying 'Flora's Ride to Horner Gate' along a track that heads across the bracken, gorse and heather of Ley Hill. This is a very pleasant route from which there are superb views to the left over the Vale of Porlock to Hurlstone Point and the villages of Bossington, Allerford and Selworthy nestling beneath the wooded slopes of Bossington Hill and Selworthy Beacon. Ahead the landscape is dominated by the familiar outline of Dunkery Beacon. This area was part of the vast Holnicote Estate of 12,000 acres, given by Sir Richard Acland to the National Trust in 1944, and many of the paths and tracks across it are named – like this one and some others used later on the walk – after members of the Acland family. Keep along the main track all the time, climbing the hill and then descending towards the Horner valley, with a fine view ahead of the thick woodland that clothes both sides of the valley.

At a T-junction of tracks turn left, shortly entering Horner Wood, and keep ahead at a footpath sign to Horner Water, heading gradually downhill through this most attractive woodland of fine old trees, mostly oak and ash, widely spaced and interspersed with delightful glades. Turn right at a footpath sign 'Granny's Ride' and after a while the path drops down to a footbridge over Horner Water where there is a footpath sign to Stoke Pero (**C**). Cross the bridge and continue steeply uphill through Stoke Wood, bearing slightly right at a footpath sign to join another path. Now the route levels out and continues to a gate. Go through and keep along the edge of the trees, continuing through another gate, along a hedge-lined path, through two more gates and onto a lane in the tiny hamlet of Stoke Pero, high up on a ridge overlooking the slopes of Dunkery Beacon (**D**). To the left is the small, sturdy-looking, plain church with a saddleback tower, mostly rebuilt at the end of the nineteenth century, which claims to be the most isolated and, at 1,013 ft (309 m), the highest church on Exmoor.

SCALE 1:25 000 or 2½ INCHES to 1 MILE

Turn right down the narrow lane and follow it for 1 mile (1.5 km), heading steeply downhill into the valley again, crossing Horner Water and turning right to head equally steeply uphill through more woodland. Continue past Wilmersham Farm, with an excellent view from here of Stoke Pero church, descending slightly to the T-junction at Pool Cross. Here turn right for a few yards and where the lane curves to the right (E) keep ahead along a broad, hedge-lined track, through a metal gate and along the right-hand edge of a field by a hedge-bank and wire fence on the right to

Isolated Stoke Pero church above the wooded slopes of the Horner valley

another metal gate. Go through that, continue along the right-hand edge of the next field, heading gradually downhill and keeping by a wire fence on the right all the time. Bear slightly right to keep above a small wooded valley on the right and then continue between hedge-banks, turning right through a metal gate. Head downhill in a straight line, later keeping along the right-hand edge of a field, to cross a footbridge over a stream. Climb a stile and continue up a steep, stony path which curves sharply left up to Lucott Farm **(F)**.

Turn left, then turn right between the farm buildings and follow the yellow-waymarked path ahead, lined with hedge-banks, passing through a gate. At a footpath sign to Porlock turn right **(G)** along the top edge of East Lucott Wood on the left and, at a yellow waymark just in front of a metal gate, bear left down to another gate. Go through and continue along the top edge of Hawk Combe, through more delightful woodland.

The next stretch of the walk is rather tortuous, so keep a sharp eye out for the indispensable but not always obvious yellow waymarks. After a while the path starts to descend and continues down in a series of curves, briefly joining a broad track before turning right, at a yellow arrow on a tree trunk, along a path that climbs again, following a series of yellow waymarks on trees. The path then drops gently downhill and just in front of a gate turns sharply left, now going more steeply downhill through a shallow valley, keeping along the side of the combe and descending steadily towards Porlock.

Finally the path leaves the woods and continues between hedges to a metal gate by the side of a house on the right. Go through and turn right for a few yards to a road. Take the left-hand fork, cross a stream and turn right at a T-junction **(H)** to follow a most pleasant lane past thatched whitewashed cottages back to Porlock church.

24 Dunkery Beacon

Start:	Webber's Post
Distance:	7½ miles (12 km). Shorter version 6 miles (9.5 km)
Approximate Time:	4 hours (3 hours for shorter version)
Parking:	Webber's Post
Refreshments:	None
Ordnance Survey maps:	Landranger 181 (Minehead & Brendon Hills area) and Pathfinder SS 84/94 1215 (Minehead)

General description *Although the highest point on Exmoor at 1704 ft (519 m), Dunkery Beacon is an easy and gradual climb from any direction and the modest amount of effort rewards you with a magnificent view, not only over a large part of Exmoor but over*

much of the surrounding countryside and coast as well. This is another of the walks on the Holnicote Estate of the Aclands, now owned by the National Trust, and many of the paths are named after members of the Acland family. The descent from Dunkery is as easy as the climb and the walk continues along the wooded valleys of Horner Water and East Water, involving some minor 'ups and downs'. Probably the stiffest climb awaits those who do the full walk — the final haul from Luccombe village back to the starting point. Although there is no real danger in bad weather conditions, this is a walk best saved for a fine day when it can be enjoyed to the full.

Refer to map overleaf.

Even the car park is attractive — situated just below Dunkery Beacon and encircled by trees. It straddles two minor, almost parallel roads and you start by walking uphill along the left-hand one of the two, signposted Dunkery Beacon, for ¼ mile (0.5 km). The road curves first to the left and then to the

Summit of Dunkery Beacon – highest point on Exmoor

right and shortly afterwards you turn right **(A)** at a footpath sign saying 'Dicky's Path to Stoke Ridge' along a path that heads across bracken and heather towards Dunkery. Descend slightly into wooded Hollow Combe, bear right and climb out of it to a crossroads of paths. Here turn left to head somewhat more steeply up a wide grassy path, bear right on joining another path and continue straight to the summit, marked by a large cairn **(B)**. As might be expected from Exmoor's highest point, the all-round views are magnificent and include the Vale of Porlock, Hurlstone Point, Selworthy, the coast of South Wales, the Quantocks and the flatter coastal lands of Somerset and Avon, Winsford Hill and Withypool Hill. In fine, clear conditions even Dartmoor, Bodmin Moor, Lundy Island, the Brecon Beacons and the Mendips can sometimes be seen.

On reaching the cairn turn right and head due west along the ridge along a path that runs nearly parallel to another one on the left, descending gently into a small hollow. At a path junction, turn right downhill, bear left on joining a broader path and follow it as it dips into Bagley Combe, crosses a stream and bends sharp right, continuing up to a road **(C)**. Turn right along the road for 1 mile (1.5 km), with superb views of the Dunkery ridge to the right, past Cloutsham Gate, from where a lane leads up to Stoke Pero, and ahead to Cloutsham Farm. Just before reaching the farm the road turns first sharp right and then left, and where it bends to the right again by the farm you turn left up to a stile **(D)**.

Climb over and a few yards ahead turn right through a gate and continue along the edge of a field, by a hedge-bank on the right. There are excellent views to the left down the steep-sided, thickly-wooded Horner valley over Porlock Vale towards Hurlstone Point. Go through a gate and continue along a broad green path, at first with a hedge-bank on the right and later keeping straight across bracken. Bear left into the woods where the path forks, following a 'Nature Trail' sign, and continue through lovely Horner Wood, turning right at the next 'Nature Trail' sign along a path that curves steeply downhill to join another path. Continue across a footbridge over East Water and shortly afterwards bear right, at a footpath sign to Webber's Post, climbing steeply to emerge from the woods and continue to a T-junction **(E)**.

At this point, walkers wishing to omit the extra 'Luccombe loop' can turn right here along a track which heads back up to Webber's Post.

Keep ahead along a narrow path, cross a track and continue into Luccombe

Plantation, following a path that curves gently to the right through the trees down to a road **(F)**. Turn left steeply downhill, under a virtual green canopy, to a crossroads where you turn right in the direction signposted Luccombe and Minehead, continuing downhill to where the road bends sharply to the left **(G)**. Here go through a kissing-gate

ahead and continue along a grassy, hedge-lined path, going through a gate and into Luccombe at the side of the church. Luccombe is another picture postcard Exmoor village: an enchanting composition of colourful thatched cottages grouped around the church. The church is an impressive and imposing building for such a

small village, with a fine, tall fifteenth-century tower.

Turn right up a narrow lane (H), passing a number of thatched cottages, and keep ahead through a gate to re-enter Luccombe Plantation. Continue along the uphill path, bearing right along the top edge of the plantation to Webber's Post.

25 'Lorna Doone Country'

Start:	Malmsmead
Distance:	8 miles (12.75 km)
Approximate Time:	4½ hours
Parking:	Malmsmead
Refreshments:	Light refreshments at Lorna Doone Farm, Malmsmead
Ordnance Survey maps:	Landranger 180 (Barnstaple & Ilfracombe) and 181 (Minehead & Brendon Hills area), Pathfinders SS 64/74 1214 (Lynton & Lynmouth) and SS 84/94 1215 (Minehead)

General description *Few walkers on Exmoor can resist the temptation to explore the valley of Badgworthy Water and the combes and open moorlands either side of it: the area that has become known as 'Lorna Doone Country'. Even without the added interest of its literary connections, it offers outstanding walking through a most atmospheric landscape of narrow, bracken-covered combes, rock-strewn streams and empty moorlands which seem to stretch away infinitely. This walk embraces all those features, and the church where, in the novel, Lorna Doone was shot. A large part of the route is across featureless moorland with few landmarks and no visible paths in many places and unless you are able to use a compass this is a walk definitely to be avoided in bad, especially misty, weather.*

Malmsmead consists of little else but the Lorna Doone Farm, overlooking the ford and picturesque old bridge over Badgworthy Water, and this is where the walk begins. Follow the direction of the sign 'Lane Leading to Public Footpath Doone Valley' along an uphill lane and where the lane bends to the right **(A)** keep ahead through a metal gate, at a public bridle-way sign to 'Doone Valley', and along a track. The track swings sharply to the left, then bears right and continues along the right-hand bank of the rock-strewn Badgworthy Water for the next 2½ miles (4 km), dipping up and down and passing through a series of gates, sometimes above and sometimes beside the stream.

After ¾ mile (1.25 km) you pass the R. D. Blackmore Memorial Stone, erected here in 1969. Boyhood holidays in the area first brought Blackmore into contact with stories

about the Doones, a gang of robbers reputed to have lived in the area in the seventeenth century. The Doones belong to the realm of legend but that is not to dispute that they may have existed — certainly people like them existed at the time. Blackmore continued to visit the area as an adult and the result was his classic novel *Lorna Doone* which, although it contains no precise locations, has become closely associated with this particular part of Exmoor.

Continue along beside the edge of the delightful and steep-sided Badgworthy Wood, with its weirdly shaped, almost contorted oak trees, and cross a footbridge; to the right is Lank Combe. As you proceed the valley becomes wilder and lonelier, its steep sides covered with rough grass and bracken. At the junction of the path to Brendon, mounds on the right covered with bracken and grass are the remains of a medieval village and to the right is Hoccombe Combe, thought by many, from the descriptions in the book, to be the real 'Doone Valley', the site of the stronghold of the legendary band of robbers, although Lank Combe (see Walk 27) also has a claim. From here continue by Badgworthy Water for another ½ mile (0.75 km) to eventually cross a footbridge **(B)**, and continue along the path on the other side, where there is a public footpath sign to Exford, bearing left uphill away from the stream over the bracken-covered expanses of Great Tom's Hill. From this path there are magnificent views over wild, open, treeless moorland, especially to the right across to the high country of The Chains. Continue across heather, and later rough grassland, to a yellow-waymarked gate in a wall. Go through it and follow the direction of a footpath sign to Tom's Hill and Alderman's Barrow across the moorland; at first there is no obvious path but keep in a straight line, heading gradually away from the wall on the left, to eventually pick up a discernible path which descends to a gate **(C)**.

Do not go through the gate but turn left and head uphill, by a hedge-bank and wire fence on the right, to a gate in the wall previously crossed. Pass through it and proceed straight ahead in a northerly direction over featureless moorland — there is an indistinct path — looking out for a gate in a wire fence in front. Go through and continue, still heading northwards in a straight line and with no path, across the rough grassland of South Common (1334 ft (407 m)). From this height there is a fine view of the coast in front. Keeping roughly parallel with the hedge-bank and line of windswept trees over to the left, look out for a metal gate in a wire fence, go through it, bear left **(D)** and head across towards the corner of a hedge-bank. Go through a gate,

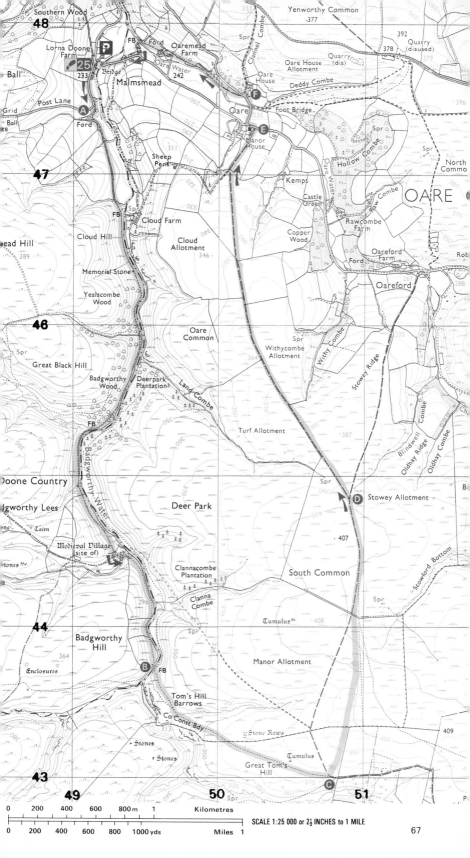

SCALE 1:25 000 or 2½ INCHES to 1 MILE

Lorna Doone Farm and old bridge over Badgworthy Water at Malmsmead

continue along the left-hand side of a hedge-bank and where it ends keep ahead, now by a wire fence and beyond that another hedge-bank on the right, along the right-hand edge of fields, passing through three gates. After the third gate bear slightly left and head downhill across a field — there is no visible path — passing through a metal gate in a wire fence and on down to a gate in the bottom left-hand corner. Go through and continue downhill, along the left-hand edge of two fields, finally passing through a gate and onto a lane (E).

Turn left past Oare church, a small, austere but dignified building. A church has stood on this site serving its widely scattered community for over 800 years and Blackmore made it the scene of one of the most dramatic events in his novel — the shooting of Lorna by Carver Doone during her wedding to Jan Ridd. Turn down the first lane on the right, signposted to Lynmouth and Porlock, cross the bridge over Oare Water and continue for 100 yards (92 m) before bearing left through a gate at a footpath sign to Malmsmead (F). Follow a pleasant, grassy, yellow-waymarked path by Oare Water, through a series of gates, along the edge of a small plantation and past Oaremead Farm on the left, finally veering right slightly uphill to a stile. Climb over, turn left downhill, recross Oare Water and continue, passing through a gate, up to a lane. Turn right back into Malmsmead.

26 Withypool and Tarr Steps

Start:	Withypool
Distance:	9½ miles (15.25 km). Shorter version 8½ miles (13.5 km)
Approximate Time:	4½ hours (3½ hours for shorter version)
Parking:	Withypool
Refreshments:	Pub at Withypool, farm café at Tarr Steps
Ordnance Survey maps:	Landranger 181 (Minehead & Brendon Hills area) and SS 83/93 1235 (Exford & Brendon Hills (West))

General description The much used and well waymarked path along the River Barle from Withypool to Tarr Steps is justifiably acclaimed as one of the finest walks in Exmoor and among the loveliest stretches of riverside walking in the country. The uniquely elaborate clapper bridge of Tarr Steps is the half-way point, the return route to Withypool first climbing above the valley and then continuing over the open moorland of Withypool Hill, passing two prehistoric sites considerably older than the clapper bridge before descending back to the village.

Although it passes through a gentle and well wooded valley, the riverside path is narrow and rocky in places and can be quite muddy; however, the climbs on the latter part of the walk are relatively undemanding.

Refer to map overleaf.

Sleepy, unpretentious and largely unchanged Withypool has the classic ingredients of a typical small English village: a medieval church which overlooks a tranquil scene of cottages, a narrow old bridge over the Barle and a cosy inn, the Royal Oak. R. D. Blackmore frequently stayed at the inn, which possesses one of his original letters, and in which he is supposed to have written at least part of *Lorna Doone*. Start by the bridge and follow the Winsford road through the village, passing the church and the Royal Oak on the left, heading uphill. Look out for a 'Two Moors Way' footpath sign on the right **(A)** where you climb a stile to begin the yellow-waymarked route to Tarr Steps; immediately there is a lovely view of the river below.

Head down to climb a stile and follow a narrow path through trees to another stile. Climb that, and another stile, descending to the river-bank to climb one more stile and cross a brook. Now hug the river-bank for the next 3½ miles (5.5 km) to Tarr Steps — a superbly attractive walk across tree-lined meadows, through woods that drop steeply down to the Barle, sometimes above and

Tarr Steps – ancient crossing over the River Barle

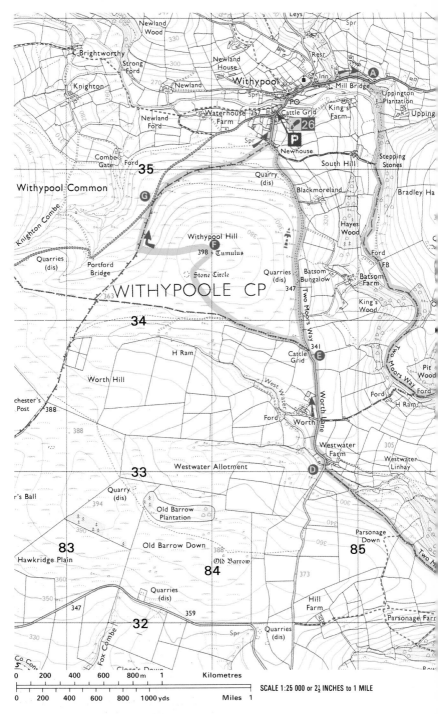

sometimes beside the river, and through a succession of stiles and gates. Yellow waymarks all the way make the route easy to follow but the path can be quite difficult in parts — muddy, narrow and rocky.

At Tarr Steps **(B)** turn right over the clapper bridge, easy enough because the large stone slabs are relatively flat and even, resting on a series of smaller stones on either side. The age of the bridge is uncertain but it

drive of the Tarr Steps Hotel and just before the hotel gates bear slightly right again along a stony, hedge-lined, uphill path, following another yellow-waymarked route to a gate. Go through and continue, curving to the right and still climbing, to go through another gate, keeping ahead along the edge of fields, with a hedge-bank on the left, on through another gate and along the edge of the next field towards Parsonage Farm.

Turn right **(C)** at a footpath sign to Withypool Hill, just before the farm, and continue along the edge of fields, by a hedge-bank on the left, climbing gently to pass through two gates. After the second one bear slightly to the right, now with a hedge-bank on the right, to a stile and gate side by side. Climb over, or go through, and continue, at a footpath sign 'Withypool via Withypool Hill', between a wire fence on the left and a line of trees on the right, descending gently to go through a metal gate. Now head across the middle of a field to go through another metal gate and turn right along a lane **(D)**, passing Westwater Farm on the right. Keep along this tree-lined lane for ½ mile (0.75 km), climbing onto the flanks of the open moorland of Withypool Hill.

Those wishing to do the slightly shorter version of the walk, omitting two prehistoric sites, can continue straight along this lane back to Withypool.

Bear left **(E)**, just after passing a cattle-grid, along a track which keeps by the edge of the open moorland, parallel to a hedge-bank on the left. Soon after the hedge-bank ends bear right and head uphill across the heather — there is no path — looking out for a circle of stones, clearly visible though of no great height. Having found the Bronze Age circle, of thirty-seven stones, bear slightly right and continue across the heather to the more easily spotted tumulus at the top of Withypool Hill (1306 ft (398 m)) **(F)**. It is gloriously fresh and open up here with the most superb all-round views. At the tumulus turn left in a westerly direction along an obvious path through the heather, heading downhill to join a broad track.

Turn right along this track to where it joins the road on the left **(G)** and at this point bear right along a path which contours around the lower slopes of the hill, keeping roughly parallel with the road on the left. There are several paths and vehicle tracks across the moorland, which can be confusing, but keep roughly parallel with the road and soon Withypool comes into view below on the left. Descend across rough grass, in the direction of a large and prominent house ahead, to join a lane by a small parking area and follow it downhill back into the village.

is probably of medieval origin, similar to but wider and much more elaborately constructed than those on Dartmoor. On the other side of the river bear right at a footpath sign to Withypool Hill, up the winding tarmac

27 County Gate, Brendon and Malmsmead Hill

Start:	County Gate
Distance:	9 miles (14.5 km)
Approximate Time:	5 hours
Parking:	County Gate

Refreshments: Light refreshments at County Gate and Malmsmead (Lorna Doone Farm), pub and tea rooms at Brendon, pub at Rockford

Ordnance Survey maps: Landranger 180 (Barnstaple & Ilfracombe) and Pathfinder SS 64/74 1214 (Lynton & Lynmouth)

```
0    200   400   600   800m   1
                              Kilometres
0    200   400   600   800   1000 yds
                              Miles    1
```

SCALE 1:25 000 or 2½ INCHES TO 1 MILE

General description *This is the second of two walks that cross part of what has become popularly known as 'Lorna Doone Country' because of its associations with R. D. Blackmore's well-known novel. It is an exceptionally fine and varied walk, beginning high up on the Devon-Somerset border, and it falls into two distinct parts. The first third is along the side of the lovely, wooded valley of the East Lyn River; the remainder, in complete contrast, is a climb over bare and open moorland — Exmoor scenery at its very finest — descending into the Badgworthy valley at Malmsmead before the final climb to*

County Gate. It is also a fairly strenuous walk, and because much of it is across open moorland with few landmarks it is best saved for a fine, clear day, when the outstanding and extensive views can be fully appreciated.

County Gate is situated high up between the moors and the sea at the point where the main road between Porlock and Lynmouth crosses the Somerset-Devon border. From the car park take the path to the right, at a footpath sign to Brendon and Malmsmead, that contours along the edge of the steep-sided valley of Ashton Cleave, with superb views to the left of Malmsmead below, the Badgworthy valley beyond and rolling moors on the horizon. Follow this most attractive path above the East Lyn River, descending slightly to go through a gate, and continue along the well defined, red-waymarked route, curving right and left, crossing a footbridge over a small brook and bearing left. Climb a stile, descend a few steps and continue, passing through a gate. Brendon can be seen ahead nestling in its sheltered valley as the path continues through two more gates and then again descends, turning sharp left over a stile and onto a lane (**A**). Bear left along the lane into Brendon.

Do not turn left over the bridge but keep ahead along the road, signposted to Lynton and Porlock, by the East Lyn, and just before the road bends to the right keep ahead, at a public footpath sign to Rockford and Watersmeet, along a riverside path which passes through a gate, crosses a field and goes through another gate by a house. For the next ¾ mile (1.25 km) keep beside or above the East Lyn along the edge of steep woodland to the right — a beautiful stretch of the route. Shortly after going through a gate turn left over the footbridge at Rockford (**B**) and turn left along the road, retracing your route but on the opposite side of the river, for ¼ mile (0.5 km). Opposite a house on the left, and at a public footpath sign to Brendon Common, turn right (**C**) onto a narrow path that heads very steeply uphill through thick woodland, by the right-hand side of a stream, to a footpath sign and onto a lane.

Turn left, following directions to 'Brendon Common via Shilstone', for about 300 yards (276 m). Where the lane bends sharply to the left (**D**) go up some steps, climb over a red-waymarked stile — there is a public footpath sign here to 'Brendon Common via Shilstone Hill' but it is difficult to see in the hedge — and continue uphill along the right-hand edge of a field, by a hedge-bank and trees on the right. At the top end of the field bear right through a gap in the hedge-bank, head straight across to Shilstone Farm, pass through a metal gate to walk through the middle of the farm buildings and on through

The view from County Gate – Exmoor at its best

another metal gate. Keep ahead for a few yards and then turn right downhill to cross a stream. Head up the other side, bearing left and continuing by a hedge-bank and wire fence on the right. Where that hedge-bank curves right keep ahead across the wide, open, heathery moorland of Shilstone Hill – the route conveniently defined by a line of red-topped posts – to the triangulation pillar at the summit (1328 ft (405 m)). From here the views are magnificent, especially ahead over the bare expanses of Brendon Common. Continue past a cairn, dropping gently to the road ahead at Dry Bridge **(E)**, situated in some of the most extensive and loneliest moorland landscape that Exmoor can offer.

Here bear left onto a broad track that curves left, bearing left again on meeting another track and continuing along it in a north-easterly direction across the heather, with superb views all around over the wild, treeless moorland. Follow this track for the next 2 miles (3.25 km), following a public bridle-way sign to Doone Valley at the first path junction and, at the second footpath sign, continuing in the direction of Malmsmead. Keep ahead at the next junction

of tracks (signposted Malmsmead and Brendon), drop down over a ford and continue (still following signs to Malmsmead and Brendon) over Malmsmead Hill to reach a lane **(F)**. Turn right along it for nearly a mile (1.5 km), heading downhill towards Malmsmead, with a glorious view of the Badgworthy valley ahead, then turn sharp left into the hamlet.

Turn right over the bridge by the Lorna Doone Farm and continue along the lane, turning left at a footpath sign to Ashton, County Gate and Oare **(G)**. Go through a metal gate, walk down a farm track, through a gate, across a footbridge over Oare Water and continue up to a stile and footpath sign. Here turn left (signposted County Gate) along a path that climbs steeply above the valley (the stream becomes the East Lyn River after the confluence of Oare Water and Badgworthy Water), with more superb views to the left over the valley, Malmsmead and the moors. After an unremitting climb between gorse and bracken, the path levels off and continues, by a wire fence on the right, passing through a gate to return to County Gate.

28 The Chains

Start:	Goat Hill Bridge
Distance:	11 miles (17.5 km)
Approximate Time:	6 hours
Parking:	Roadside parking areas near Goat Hill Bridge
Refreshments:	None
Ordnance Survey maps:	Landranger 180 (Barnstaple & Ilfracombe) and Pathfinder SS 64/74 1214 (Lynton & Lynmouth)

General description *The wilderness of The Chains is one of the most extensive areas of open, unenclosed moorland remaining on Exmoor and one of the most elevated, rising to nearly 1600 ft (487 m). Its boggy heartland is the source of many of Exmoor's rivers and streams — the Exe, Barle, West Lyn and Hoaroak Water — and it was heavy rains on The Chains in August 1952 that was responsible for the devastation of Lynmouth, as well as much damage elsewhere in the locality. For the fit and experienced rambler it provides outstanding walking: the views are magnificent and the feeling of freedom and spaciousness, even of mystery, is exhilarating. But the paths are not always clear and the going can be rough at times. Unless you are skilled in the use of a compass this is definitely a walk to be avoided in bad, especially misty, weather; but in fine and clear conditions it is one that will remain in the memory for a long time.*

Refer to map overleaf.

From the parking area, turn west along the main road over Goat Hill Bridge. Soon after crossing the county boundary, turn right onto a bridle-way **(A)** and follow it for 1 mile (1.5 km) to the junction of paths at Woodbarrow Gate, keeping to the right of a bank. Wood Barrow is the prominent mound, one of the numerous tumuli in the area.

At a footpath sign to Barbrook, go through a metal gate in the Chains Wall **(B)** (the open country of The Chains lies to the north of the boundary wall), and head straight across the moorland. The path is not always clear but keep in a straight line — there is a lovely view ahead of the West Lyn valley and coast beyond — descending towards a line of trees and metal gate in a wall ahead (Saddle Gate) **(C)**.

Go through and follow the well defined track, signposted to Barbrook, as far as Shallowford **(D)**. Opposite the farm cottage turn right and take the bridle-way which heads eastwards across open moorland, through an area of cairns and tumuli, to drop down and pass through a gate at Hill Cottage **(E)**. Continue to North Furzehill, using a new track to bypass the farmyard, and keep along the tarmac lane, turning right through a metal gate **(F)** after a sharp left-hand bend.

Now follow a bridle-way, initially between banks, but after passing through a wooden gate keep them on your left. Continue through two more gates and then the path, signposted to Hoaroak, turns sharply to the right **(G)**. Go through a gap in the wall and continue across Furzehill Common into the lovely but lonely valley of Hoaroak Water. The route is not very clear at this point but there are red waymarks to guide you across this wild and open landscape to Hoaroak **(H)**, after which the path becomes easily visible, keeping by Hoaroak Water on the left. After crossing a small stream, continue through a gate in the wall to a footpath sign a few yards ahead. To the left, on the other side of the stream, is the Hoar Oak Tree (with a fence around it), an ancient boundary marker of the medieval Exmoor Forest. The original tree disappeared a long time ago and the present

Pinkworthy Pond amid the wild country of The Chains

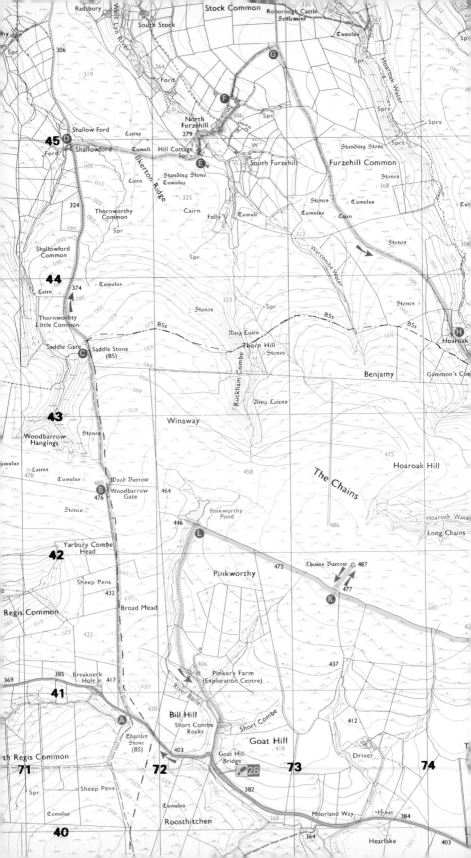

one is the latest of a whole series of successors.

Continue, following directions to Exe Head, along a path above Hoaroak Water on the left; cross the water where it turns right into Long Chains Combe and keep ahead above another stream, this time on the right, climbing steadily to Exe Head **(J)**. As its name suggests, this is near the source of Exmoor's major river and a tremendous viewpoint — especially to the left across the bare expanses of Exe Plain.

At Exe Head you regain the Chains Wall. Go through a gate in the wall, turn right at a footpath sign to Chains Barrow, Pinkworthy Pond and Cornham, pass through two gates and continue along the left-hand side of the Chains Wall for 1¼ miles (2 km). At the next footpath sign keep ahead, following directions to Chains Barrow and Pinkworthy Pond, continuing beside the wall and through

two more gates to the next footpath sign **(K)**. Here turn right through a gate for a short detour along an often boggy path to Chains Barrow, clearly visible ahead topped by a triangulation pillar. This is the highest point on The Chains at 1598 ft (487 m) and provides one of the most magnificent views on Exmoor: looking northwards to the North Devon coast, eastwards to Dunkery Beacon, southwards over rolling expanses of moorland and westwards across the farmlands of mid-Devon.

Return to the gate in the Chains Wall **(K)** and keep along by the wall for another ½ mile (0.75 km) to Pinkworthy Pond **(L)**, source of the River Barle. It is in fact a small reservoir, built by the Knight family who reclaimed much of Exmoor in the nineteenth century, but its exact purpose remains a mystery.

Turn left at a footpath sign, by a gate in the Chains Wall, along an obvious path which descends gently, and pass through another gate. From here the way ahead is not always visible on the ground but the route is easy to follow as there are plenty of yellow waymarks. Keeping the infant River Barle to the right, go through a gap in a hedge-bank, then through another and continue along a grassy path to a footpath sign near farm buildings on the left.

This is Pinkery Farm, which has been developed as an exploration centre for schoolchildren. The farm was part of the Pinkworthy Estate which, following successful protests about plans in 1958 to plant conifers on The Chains, was bought by Somerset County Council in 1969 in order to provide public access and preserve the existing landscape. At the footpath sign turn right and walk along the drive, still by the Barle on the right, to Goat Hill Bridge and the starting point.

The last part of this walk, from Exe Head to Pinkworthy Pond and on to Goat Hill Bridge, follows Exmoor National Park permissive paths which may be closed from time to time in the interests of conservation. If these paths are closed, an alternative route can be followed from point (J) using a public right of way. Go through a gate in the Chains Wall, turn right and pass through two more gates. After the second gate, bear left off the track and head across a boggy field — the path here is unclear but follows a south-westerly direction, crossing three small streams. Make for a gate with a red waymark, go through, continue to another gate in the wall ahead, and after passing through that the path becomes clearly marked. Head across a field to a sheep-fold, pass through it and continue down to the road. Turn right to return to Goat Hill Bridge.

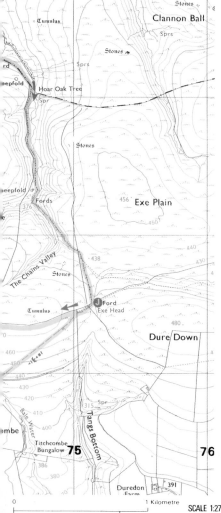

SCALE 1:27 174

Useful organisations

The Countryside Commission,
John Dower House, Crescent Place,
Cheltenham, Gloucestershire GL50 3RA.
Tel: 0242 21381

The National Trust,
36 Queen Anne's Gate, London
SW1H 9AS. Tel: 071-222 9251
(Wessex Regional Office, Stourton,
Warminster, Wiltshire BA12 6QD.
Tel: 0747 840 224
Devon Regional Office, Killerton House,
Broadclyst, Exeter EX5 3LE.
Tel: 0392 881691)

Council for National Parks,
45 Shelton Street, London WC2H 9HS.
Tel: 071-240 3603

Exmoor National Park,
Exmoor House, Dulverton, Somerset
TA22 9HL. Tel: 0398 23665

National Park Authority Visitor Centres can
be found at:
Dulverton (Tel: 0398 23665)
Dunster (Tel: 0643 821835)
County Gate (Tel: 05987 321)
Lynmouth (Tel: 0598 52509)
Combe Martin (Tel: 027 188 3319)

West Country Tourist Board,
Trinity Court, Southernhay East, Exeter
EX1 1QS. Tel: 0392 76351

Exmoor Society,
Middle Cleave, Northam, Bideford,
Devon EX39 2RJ. Tel: 023 72 77959

The Ramblers' Association,
1/5 Wandsworth Road, London
SW8 2LJ. Tel: 071-582 6878

The Forestry Commission,
Information Branch, 231 Corstorphine
Road, Edinburgh EH12 7AT.
Tel: 031 334 0303

The Youth Hostels Association,
Trevelyan House, 8 St Stephen's Hill,
St Albans, Hertfordshire, AL1 2DY.
Tel: 0727 55215

The Long Distance Walkers' Association,
Lodgefield Cottage, High Street,
Wadhurst, East Sussex TN5 7PH.
Tel: 058 087 341

The Council for the Protection of Rural
England,
4 Hobart Place, London SW1W 0HY.
Tel: 071-235 5959

Ordnance Survey,
Romsey Road, Maybush, Southampton
SO9 4DH. Tel: 0703 792764/5 or 792749

Ordnance Survey maps of Exmoor

Exmoor is covered by Ordnance Survey
1:50 000 (1¼ inches to 1 mile) scale
Landranger map sheets 180 and 181. These
all-purpose maps are packed with
information to help you explore the area.
Viewpoints, picnic sites, places of interest,
caravan and camping sites are shown, as well
as public rights of way information such as
footpaths and bridle-ways.

To examine Exmoor in more detail and
especially if you are planning walks,
Ordnance Survey Pathfinder maps at
1:25 000 (2½ inches to 1 mile) scale are ideal.

Maps covering this area are:

1213 (SS 44/54/14)	1254 (SS 42/52)
1214 (SS 64/74)	1255 (SS 62/72)
1215 (SS 84/94)	1256 (SS 82/92)
1233 (SS 43/53)	1274 (SS 41/51)
1234 (SS 63/73)	1275 (SS 61/71)
1235 (SS 83/93)	1276 (SS 81/91)

Tourists will also find the Touring Map of
Exmoor 5 and the Touring Map and Guide of
The West Country 13 useful. These maps
provide lots of helpful information so that
visitors can make the most of their stay.

To get to Exmoor, use the Ordnance
Survey Routemaster map number 8 South
West England and South Wales at 1:250 000
(1 inch to 4 miles) scale.

Ordnance Survey maps and guides are
available from most booksellers, stationers
and newsagents.

Index